ASIAPAC BOOKS

The TAO Inspiration

Illustrated by Feng Ge   Translated by Yang Liping

ASIAPAC • SINGAPORE

Publisher
ASIAPAC BOOKS PTE LTD
996 Bendemeer Road #06-09
Singapore 339944
Tel: (65) 6392 8455
Fax: (65) 6392 6455
Email: asiapacbooks@pacific.net.sg

Come visit us at our Internet home page
www.asiapacbooks.com

First published June 2005
2nd edition January 2008

© 2005 ASIAPAC BOOKS, SINGAPORE
ISBN 13 978-981-229-396-1
ISBN 10   981-229-396-5

Publisher: Lim Li Kok
Publishing director: Lydia Lum
Project editor: Seah Bee Bee
Preface & appendix: Zhou Jue Jing
Artwork & cover illustrations: Feng Ge
Cover design: Thomas Terh
Page layout: Kelly Lim
Body text: 11pt Avant Garde Md BT
Printer: Loi Printing Pte Ltd

Publisher's Note

The Tao Inspiration is a beautifully illustrated book designed to present the ancient Chinese classic *Tao Te Ching* in a plain and inspirational style. It aims to help you understand the great ancient Chinese metaphysical wisdom in a friendly and thought-provoking way, and guide you to tease out each and every profound thought and apply it to your daily life.

We have also compiled an index called "The Essence of Tao" on some key terms reflecting Lao Zi's thought. They are *wu-wei* or non-interference, *zi-ran* or nature, *rou-ruo* or soft and weak, and *bu-zheng* or non-competitive. The purpose is to help readers better understand Lao Zi's philosophy in a practical way.

Asiapac would like to thank Chen Wangheng, Professor of Aesthetics and PhD supervisor with Department of Philosophy, Wuhan University, and Feng Ge, the illustrator, for their painstaking efforts. At the same time, Asiapac is also appreciative of Master Lee Zhiwang, President of Singapore Taoist Mission, who graces this book with an excellent foreword.

Lastly, we would like to extend our thanks to everyone in the editorial team who has contributed to the production of this book. And to the readers, we wish you experience much enlightenment through the wisdom and philosophies of Lao Zi, and enjoy a fulfilling and meaningful life.

Foreword

I am truly encouraged and pleased that Asiapac Books Pte Ltd has put together this informative book based on Lao Zi's *Tao Te Ching*, adding to their publications on Chinese philosophy and wisdom which have been well received worldwide.

The editing team has come up with beautifully illustrated drawings to present the deep philosophies of Lao Zi in an innovative and a more reader-friendly way. In this way, the Sage's wisdom can be an inspiration to more people.

The launch of *The Tao Inspiration* is timely. In our turbulent world today, Lao Zi's profound philosophies of "Tao" and "Virtues", which adhere to the law of nature, will help one find peace with oneself and bring harmony to the society.

I wish Asiapac Books Pte Ltd all the best in reaching out to the masses through their meaningful and creative works.

"Fu Sheng Wu Liang Tian Zun (福生无量天尊). *"* May heavenly blessings be with you and always cherish the Three Treasures that Lao Zi has given to us, compassion, frugality and humility.

Master Lee Zhiwang
President
Taoist Mission (Singapore)
29 April 2005

About the Illustrator

Feng Ge was born in 1973 in Yuechi of Sichuan province, China. He graduated from the Art College of the Xinan Shifan University, specialising in oil painting. He is currently working in a comics studio in Shanghai.

He has loved drawing since his childhood days. In 1995, he started working on comics, and he has since produced *The Seven Lads of Yang*, *Celestial Eagle of the Snow*, *Flute Sage*, *The Curtain of Heaven Falls*, *The Sword of Sorrow*, and *Wild Goose on Goat's Sand*. In 2004, he also produced the award-winning comic, *Tao Te Ching*.

About the Translator

Yang Liping is currently a PhD candidate at the Department of English Language and Literature, National University of Singapore, doing his research on the influence of translated foreign texts on the making of modern Chinese culture.

He has worked as a full-time translator at the Central Compilation and Translation Bureau (based in Beijing) for seven years. His main interest is in literary translation and cultural exchange between China and the West in the pre-modern and modern periods.

To date, he has published articles on Eugene O'Neil and Flannery O'Conner as well as more than 10 book translations, including *Midnight in the Garden of Good & Evil* (1997), *The British Museum is Falling Down* (1998), *Digital Capitalism* (2001), *Nicolae – the Rise of Antichrist* (2001), *Apollyon* (2002), *Modern Chinese Drama* (1999), *Catastrophe of the 20th Century* (2000), and *Old Cultural Works* (Cambridge Poetry Translation Series, 2002).

He also translated *Gateway to Eurasian Culture*, *Gateway to Chinese Literature* and *Origins of Chinese Science and Technology* for Asiapac Books.

Contents

Introduction

"A journey of a thousand miles begins with a single step."
"Heaven and Earth endure."
"Superior skills look clumsy."
"Governance based on non-intervention."
"Being and nothingness create each other."
"You are a wise person if you know yourself."

Many aphorisms, like those listed above, contain almost perfect wisdom and inspiring metaphysical meanings. They came from an ancient Chinese classic. Some say it is a book on life; others believe it is a discourse on military affairs, still others view it as a book about *qigong*. There are even people who have teased out from it concepts of mathematics and natural sciences. It presents a different face to everyone. What book is this?

It is a Chinese classic that was written 2,500 years ago — *Tao Te Ching*. What kind of book is it? What does it tell us? How should we read it?

Background information on *Tao Te Ching*

Lao Zi is said to be China's first important philosopher and thinker who lived over 2,000 years ago. His work, *Tao Te Ching*, though containing only 5,000 Chinese characters, was first to express the philosophy that man and nature should coexist in balance. This has exerted considerable influence on the history of China as a whole.

Tao Te Ching, also known as *A Treatise of Five Thousand Characters* or *Lao Zi*, covers a wide range of subject matter, including politics, philosophy, military affairs, art, health, psychology and ethics. Today, the book has many different editions. There are more than 100 ancient editions. Of these, the edition annotated by Wang Bi (AD 226–249) and the silk edition unearthed from a Han Dynasty tomb at Mai-wang-dui in Changsha in 1974 are most valued by the academic world.

Tao Te Ching contains 81 chapters. The chapter structure is not seen in the original script, as it was later added by some Taoists in the Eastern Han Dynasty. The structure was preserved in the Wang Bi edition and is still in use today.

Tao Te Ching is an immortal work, which is regarded by scholars in Japan, the former Soviet Union, Germany, United Kingdom and many other countries as a unique ancient philosophical classic. Lao Zi was also nominated by the *New York Times* as one of the Top 10 writers of the ancient world. The classic has produced a far-reaching influence on the intellectual and cultural development of China and the world as well.

Introduction to the Content of *Tao Te Ching*

It is well known that *Tao Te Ching* is a classic which is pithy in diction and profound in implication. How should we approach it both textually and ideationally? In analysing the textual meaning, it is also important to understand Lao Zi's thought. It is this system of thought that is the reason the book has endured over the past 2,000 years.

Tao Te Ching is divided into two parts: Tao Ching (The Classic of Tao) and Te Ching (The Classic of Virtue). Tao is something that is invisible yet real and present. The first 37 chapters comprise the Tao Ching and the remaining chapters constitute the Te Ching. Te or Virtue is the human manifestations of Tao.

1. The Central Concept of Tao Te Ching – Tao

Textual Interpretation

As the central concept of *Tao Te Ching*, the character of "Tao" appears about 70 times throughout the book (see Appendix 1). It has three different meanings:

First, it is used as a verb meaning "to utter; to articulate" as in "Tao, if articulable, is not the eternal Tao" (Chapter 1). Second, it means "the way" as in "The bright path looks dark, / Advancing seems retreating, / And the flat path looks bumpy" (Chapter 41). The third meaning points to the quintessential and also the most unique part of *Tao Te Ching*—something pure, simple and immaterial as embodied by terms such as "the beginning of Heaven and Earth," and "the mother of the myriad things in the world". This is the core meaning around which the whole text revolves.

Ideational Interpretation
First, it refers to the way of everything in the world. It is not visible but it exists beyond doubt, giving birth to everything between Heaven and Earth.
Second, it refers to objective law. Everything in the world is subject to the law of mutual opposition and recurrence. The law also governs human conduct.
Third, it signifies the actual way of life. When it translates to codes of human conduct, Tao becomes Te or Virtue. Te is the specific embodiment of Tao's spirit and nature—spontaneous, non-interfering, empty, serene, soft, weak, simple, non-competitive, peaceful, indifferent to fame, pure, and unadorned.

2. The Vital Concept of *Tao Te Ching* – Te or Virtue: non-interfering, spontaneous, empty, serene, soft and weak.

For Lao Zi, all human struggle and conflict arise from men's competitiveness, conceit and self-importance. Thus, men should keep a "soft and weak", "modest" and "non-competitive" mind, and refrain from pursuing fame and gain. Only then can they resolve all conflicts and disputes, and become morally cultivated.

The Legend
of Lao Zi

The imposing Hangu Pass was a renowned fortress of great strategic importance during the Spring and Autumn Period.
One morning, after a night rain, mist rose in the valley. Yin Xi, the warden of Hangu Pass was a skilled astrologer, and seeing the mist coil like dragons in the east, cried, "A sage will travel west through this pass!"

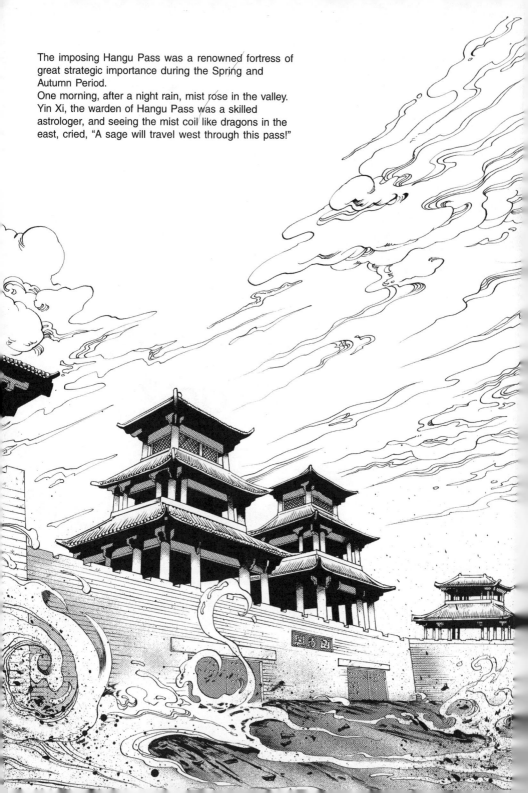

Indeed, a few days later, a dark ox carrying an old man slowly walked up. The old man looked kind and unaffected. Yin Xi immediately recognised him as the sage Lao Zi.

Lao Zi's full name was Li Er, with the literary name Boyang, and he was also known as Lao Dan. He lived in Queren village (present-day Luyi county in Henan) during the Spring and Autumn Period.

Legend has it that Lao Zi's mother became pregnant after a meteor entered her body. She remained pregnant for 72 years (81 years according to another source), before Lao Zi was born from her left underarm. Being grey-haired at birth, he was named Lao Zi (literally meaning "old son"). When he was born, Lao Zi pointed at a nearby plum tree (pronounced "Li" in Chinese) and declared, "That is my family name." Hence, he is surnamed Li.

Lao Zi's birthplace has been a contentious subject for long. In recent years, scholars claimed that based on archaeological findings, Lao Zi's hometown should be in Woyang County of Anhui Province in China.

Lao Zi was once a historiographer in charge of the court archives. His knowledge of the social and historical matters was unsurpassed and well-known throughout the land.

One day, the great educator Confucius came to visit Lao Zi. Lao Zi left the city to welcome him in person. In accordance to the etiquette of the time, Confucius respectfully presented Lao Zi with a wild goose.

Confucius questioned Lao Zi on many issues, and Lao Zi replied cogently to all of them.
At their parting, Lao Zi had these words of wisdom for Confucius: "What you are studying is all handed down from the past. Do not take them as golden rules set in stone.
"Secondly, a gentleman should take an official post at an appropriate time, and retire when it is no longer appropriate.

"Thirdly, a man of learning and virtue is still and sombre, without display. A gentleman overflowing with virtue appears foolish on the surface."

Lao Zi's words struck home to Confucius' weaknesses. Confucius thanked him profusely and left in silence. For three days after his return, he did not hold classes. His disciples were confused.

Confucius sighed, "Birds can fly. Fish can swim. Beasts can run. Those that run can be snared with nets; those that swim can be caught on a line; those that fly can be brought down with arrows.

But dragons I cannot know. They ride the wind and clouds and ascend into the heavens. Lao Zi, whom I met, is like a dragon."

Yi Xin begged Lao Zi to write down his thoughts. Lao Zi declined several times, but was eventually moved by his sincerity. Lao Zi picked up his brush and began to write...

Out of respect for Lao Zi, Yi Xin humbly begged his teaching and they spent much time discussing the Tao.

Lao Zi then continued to write, and finally completed his marvellous work. Filled with profound meaning and encompassing Heaven, Earth and the Universe in its scope — this is the *Tao Te Ching*.

The *Tao Te Ching* is also known as *Discourse of 5,000 Characters* and *Laozi*, and is divided into two parts. Part One concerns Tao, inquiring into the fundamentals of the universe and the laws governing changes, while Part Two elaborates on Virtue, concerning how men act in society. As the pioneering first complete work of Chinese philosophy, the *Tao Te Ching* has provided inspiration on moral, personal and state levels.

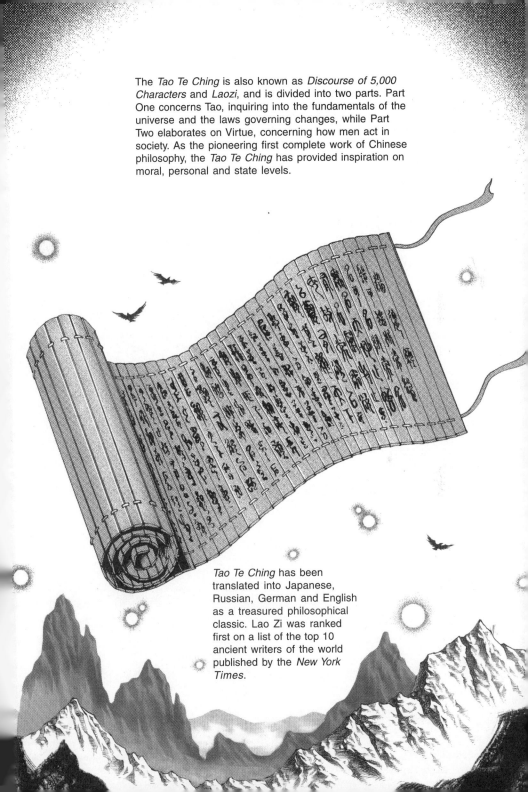

Tao Te Ching has been translated into Japanese, Russian, German and English as a treasured philosophical classic. Lao Zi was ranked first on a list of the top 10 ancient writers of the world published by the *New York Times*.

Tao Te Ching

Tao Te Ching
Chapter 1

Tao, if articulable, is not the eternal Tao.
The name, if can be named, is not the eternal name.
Heaven and earth start with no name,
The named is the mother of everything under the sun.
Thus, with a detached mind, you see the secret,
With an interested mind, you see the appearances.
These two grow out of the same,
But they are named differently.
They are both mysterious.
Mysterious and ineffable,
They are the essence of all secrets.

《道德经》第一章
dào dé jīng dì yī zhāng

道 可 道，非 常 道；名 可 名，非 常 名。
dào kě dào fēi cháng dào míng kě míng fēi cháng míng

无 名 天 地 之 始；有 名 万 物 之 母。
wú míng tiān dì zhī shǐ yǒu míng wàn wù zhī mǔ

故 常 无，欲 以 观 其 妙；常 有，欲 以 观 其 徼。
gù cháng wú yù yǐ guān qí miào cháng yǒu yù yǐ guān qí jiào

此 两 者，同 出 而 异 名，同 谓 之 玄。
cǐ liǎng zhě tóng chū ér yì míng tóng wèi zhī xuán

玄 之 又 玄，众 妙 之 门。
xuán zhī yòu xuán zhòng miào zhī mén

15

Tao Te Ching
Chapter 2

Ugliness arises
When everybody knows what is beautiful.
Evil emerges
When all recognises what is good.
Thus, being and nothingness create each other.
Difficulty and ease depend on each other.
Long and short are relative.
High and low are mutually inclusive.
Sound and voice are harmonious.
Front and back follow each other.
Thus the sage acts effortlessly,
And teaches not by words.
The myriad things rise and fall unobstructed.
The world is created but not possessed,
Deeds are performed yet not for ostentation.
This is accomplishing without pretension.
Because of such non-pretension,
The accomplishments will never be removed.

《道 德 经》 第 二 章
dào dé jīng dì èr zhāng

天 下 皆 知 美 之 为 美，斯 恶 已；
tiān xià jié zhī měi zhī wéi měi sī wù yǐ

皆 知 善 之 为 善，斯 不 善 已。
jié zhī shàn zhī wéi shàn sī bú shàn yǐ

有 无 相 生，难 易 相 成，长 短 相 形，
yǒu wú xiāng shēng nán yì xiāng chéng cháng duǎn xiāng xíng

高 下 相 盈，音 声 相 和，前 后 相 随，恒 也。
gāo xià xiāng yíng yīn shēng xiāng hé qián hòu xiāng suí héng yě

是 以 圣 人 处 无 为 之 事，行 不 言 之 教；
shì yǐ shèng rén chǔ wú wéi zhī shì xíng bù yán zhī jiào

万 物 作 而 弗 始，生 而 弗 有，为 而 弗 恃，功 成 而 弗 居。
wàn wù zuò ér fú shǐ shēng ér fú yǒu wéi ér fú shì gōng chéng ér fú jū

夫 唯 弗 居，是 以 不 去。
fū wéi fú jū shì yǐ bú qù

Everything in the world is subject to the universal law of unity of opposites.

To resolve the conflicts, a strategy that stresses autonomy and non-interference should be adopted.

17

Tao Te Ching
Chapter 3

If the worthy is not exalted,
You will not create competition among people.
If rarities are not valued,
You will have no trouble of theft.
If desirable things are kept out of sight,
People will remain calm and unperturbed.
Therefore, when the sage governs a country,
He clarifies the people's minds,
Fills their bellies,
Dilutes their desires,
And strengthens their bones.
When the people remain guileless and desireless,
Clever men dare not act recklessly.
If you act without striving,
Nothing is beyond manageability.

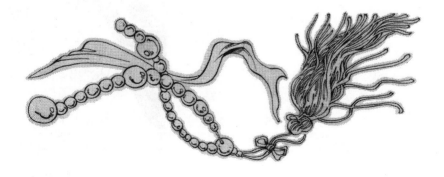

《道德经》第三章
dào dé jīng dì sān zhāng

不尚贤，使民不争；不贵难得之货，使民不为盗；
bú shàng xián shǐ mín bù zhēng bú guì nán dé zhī huò shǐ mín bù wéi dào

不见可欲，使民心不乱。
bú xiàn kě yù shǐ mín xīn bú luàn

是以圣人之治，虚其心，实其腹，弱其志，强其骨。
shì yǐ shèng rén zhī zhì xū qí xīn shí qí fù ruò qí zhì qiáng qí gǔ

常使民无知无欲。使夫智者不敢为也。
cháng shǐ mín wú zhī wú yù shǐ fū zhì zhě bù gǎn wéi yě

为无为，则无不治。
wéi wú wéi zé wú bú zhì

Social stability calls for a government founded on the principle of non-interference.

19

Tao Te Ching
Chapter 4

Tao is void and shapeless,
Yet its power unlimited.
So profound; it is the origin
of the myriad things!
It blunts their sharpness,
Dim and intangible, it is
present.
I do not know what it is like.
It seems to have existed
before the ancestors of the
emperors.

《道德经》 第四章
dào dé jīng　dì sì zhāng

道 冲，而 用 之 或 不 盈。
dào chōng ér yòng zhī huò bù yíng

渊 兮，似 万 物 之 宗；湛 兮，似 或 存。
yuān xī　sì wàn wù zhī zōng　shèn xī　sì huò cún

吾 不 知 谁 之 子，象 帝 之 先。
wū bù zhī shuí zhī zi　xiàng dì zhī xiān

21

Tao Te Ching
Chapter 5

Heaven and Earth are not benevolent,
The myriad things come and go like straw dogs.
The sage is not benevolent
The masses live and die naturally like straw dogs.
The space between Heaven and Earth,
Isn't it like a bellows?
It is empty yet inexhaustible.
Push it and more will come out.
The more you say, the poorer you are.
It is better to keep to the centre.

《道 德 经》 第 五 章
dào dé jīng dì wǔ zhāng

天 地 不 仁，以 万 物 为 刍 狗；
tiān dì bù rén yǐ wàn wù wéi chú gǒu

圣 人 不 仁，以 百 姓 为 刍 狗。
shèng rén bù rén yǐ bǎi xìng wéi chú gǒu

天 地 之 间，其 犹 橐 龠 乎！
tiān dì zhī jiān qí yóu tuó yuè hū

虚 而 不 屈，动 而 愈 出。多 言 数 穷，不 如 守 中。
xū ér bù qū dòng ér yù chū duō yán shù qióng bù rú shǒu zhōng

The ideal rulers should comply with the natural law by adopting a policy of non-interference; which allows the people to work, rest, hire and die in their own ways with being interfered at all.

Tao Te Ching
Chapter 6

The valley spirit never dies,
It is called the mysterious mother.
The ovary of the mysterious mother
Is called the root of Heaven and Earth.
Continuous and intangible,
It is inexhaustible.

《道德经》 第六章
dào dé jīng　dì liù zhāng

谷神不死，是谓玄牝。
gǔ shén bù sǐ　shì wèi xuán pìn

玄牝之门，是谓天地根。
xuán pìn zhī mén　shì wèi tiān dì gēn

绵绵若存，用之不勤。
mián mián ruò cún yòng zhī bù qín

25

Tao Te Ching
Chapter 7

Heaven and Earth endure.
The reason they do so
Is that they do not live for themselves,
And thus they can endure.
The sage puts himself behind and ends up in the front.
He exposes himself and ends up a safe survivor.
He establishes himself because of his selflessness.

《道德经》第七章
dào dé jīng dì qī zhāng

天长地久。
tiān cháng dì jiǔ

天地所以能长且久者，
tiān dì suǒ yi néng cháng qiě jiǔ zhě

以其不自生，故能长生。
yi qí bú zì shēng gù néng cháng shēng

是以圣人后其身而身先；
shì yi shèng rén hòu qí shēn ér shēn xiān

外其身而身存。
wài qí shēn ér shēn cún

非以其无私邪? 故能成其私。
fēi yi qí wú sī yé gù néng chéng qí sī

People in power tend to take advantage of every opportunity to satisfy their strong desire to possess. The sage does not put his personal interests before the people's. He does not think about things from his personal perspective. As such, he can obtain the support of the people.

Tao Te Ching
Chapter 8

Ultimate kindness is like water.
Water benefits rather than rivals with everything.
Such a person resides in a place hideous to all.
He is thus close to Tao.
He inhabits the lowland;
His mind is as calm as the abyss,
He associates with others kindly,
He honours his words,
He governs well,
He handles affairs properly,
He never lets go of good opportunities,
Since he does not compete,
He is free of errors.

《道德经》第八章
dào dé jīng dì bā zhāng

上善若水。
shàng shàn ruò shuǐ

水善利万物而不争，
shuǐ shàn lì wàn wù ér bù zhēng

处众人之所恶，故几于道。
chǔ zhòng rén zhī suǒ wù gù jǐ yú dào

居善地，心善渊，与善仁，
jū shàn dì xīn shàn yuān yú shàn rén

言善信，政善治，事善能，动善时。
yán shàn xìn zhèng shàn zhì shì shàn néng dòng shàn shí

夫唯不争，故无尤。
fū wéi bù zhēng gù wú yóu

Because he does not rival with others he will not run into serious trouble. The top virtue should be like water. Firstly, it is gentle; secondly, it resides in lower places; and thirdly, it nourishes rather than rivals with everything. A man of integrity not only does things that benefit people, but also offers to go to places people do not like to go. He is also ready to make the utmost effort to do whatever people hate to do.

Tao Te Ching
Chapter 9

Having more than enough,
Is worse than having nothing.
A knife sharpened too much,
Does not last long.
A house full of gold and jadestones,
Cannot be guarded for long.
A pretentious man of means,
Incurs misfortunes.
Retire upon achieving success,
This is the way of heaven.

《道德经》第九章
dào dé jīng dì jiǔ zhāng

持而盈之，不如其已；
chí ér yíng zhī bù rú qí yǐ

揣而锐之，不可长保。
chuǎi ér ruì zhī bù kě cháng bǎo

金玉满堂，莫之能守；
jīn yù mǎn táng mò zhī néng shǒu

富贵而骄，自遗其咎。
fù guì ér jiāo zì yí qí jiù

功遂身退，天之道也。
gōng suí shēn tuì tiān zhī dào yě

Whatever you do, remember to refrain from going to extremes. You should stop at an appropriate moment. Excesses, such as showing off your abilities, becoming arrogant after getting rich, claiming credit for yourself and clinging to high positions, will surely get you into trouble.

Tao Te Ching
Chapter 10

When body and soul come together,
Will they be separated someday?
Concentrating your mind till suppleness is achieved,
Can you become like an infant?
Cleansing your mind,
Are you free of defects?
Ruling the state with a kind heart,
Can you achieve non-interference?
When the gate of Heaven opens and closes,
Can you remain calm and silent as a female?
If you are sensible and clear-eyed,
Can you go without knowledge?

《道德经》第十章
dào dé jīng dì shí zhāng

载营魄抱一，能无离乎？专气致柔，能如婴儿乎？
zāi yín pò bào yī néng wú lí hū zhuān qì zhì róu néng rú yīng ér hū

涤除玄鉴，能如疵乎？爱国治民，能无为乎？
dí chú xuán jiàn néng rú chī hū ài guó zhì mín néng wú wéi hū

天门开阖，能为雌乎？明白四达，能无知乎？
tiān mén kāi hé néng wéi cí hū míng bái sì dá néng wú zhī hū

Maintain a balance between the body and the soul. Protect the mind from being disturbed and contaminated by various desires and prejudices. In addition, work hard to understand the law of nature and step up moral cultivation so as to rule the state with a people-loving heart.

33

Tao Te Ching
Chapter 11

Thirty spokes converge at the hub,
A cart becomes useful
Because of the hole in the centre.
A vessel is made of clay,
The vessel is useful because of the emptiness within.
A house is built when doors and windows are made,
It functions as a house because of the empty spaces within the walls.
Thus, what is present is beneficial,
And what is absent is useful.

《道德经》第十一章
dào dé jīng dì shí yī zhāng

三十辐，共一毂，当其无，有车之用。
sān shí fú gòng yì gǔ dāng qí wú yǒu chē zhī yòng

埏埴以为器，当其无，有器之用。
yán zhí yǐ wéi qì dàng qí wú yǒu qì zhī yòng

凿户牖以为室，当其无，有室之用。
záo hù yǒu yǐ wéi shì dāng qí wú yǒu shì zhī yòng

故有之以为利，无之以为用。
gù yǒu zhī yǐ wéi lì wú zhī yǐ wéi yòng

We tend to focus our attention on things tangible and their functions, and neglect what is empty and its functions.

Presence and absence are interdependent. What is absent may also play an important part, only that it usually goes unnoticed.

Tao Te Ching
Chapter 12

The five colours make our eyes blind.
The five musical tones make our ears deaf.
The five flavours spoil our taste.
Our minds are out of control when hunting on horseback.
Rare treasures in hand debase our conduct.
Therefore, the sage prefers food to beauty.
He abandons that for this.

《道德经》第十二章
dào dé jīng dì shí èr zhāng

五色令人目盲；
wǔ sè lìng rén mù máng

五音令人耳聋；
wu yīn lìng rén ér lóng

五味令人口爽；
wǔ wèi lìng rén kǒu shuǎng

驰骋畋猎，令人心发狂；
chí chěng tián liè lìng rén xīn fā kuáng

难得之货，令人行妨。
nán dé zhī huò lìng rén xíng fáng

是以圣人为腹不为目，故去彼取此。
shì yǐ shèng rén wéi fù bù wéi mù gù qù bǐ qǔ cǐ

A man will end up in disgrace if he is caught up in the five colours, five tones and five flavours, and indulges himself in racing and hunting.

Therefore, the sage only wants to fill his belly while at the same time preventing his eyes from being tempted by the material world.

Tao Te Ching
Chapter 13

Accept honour and disgrace as a surprise,
Value great misfortunes as you value your self.
What does "Accept honour and disgrace as a surprise" means?
Honour is respected,
Disgrace disregarded.
Surprised to get either of them
And also surprised to lose either of them.
That's what "Accept honour and disgrace as a surprise" means.
What do I mean by "Value great misfortunes as you value your self"?
I will go through misfortunes
Because I have a body.
If I am without a body,
What misfortunes do I have?
Therefore, if you dedicate yourself to the world,
You can be entrusted with the world.
If you love to serve the world with your self,
You can truly uphold the world.

《道 德 经》 第 十 三 章
dào dé jīng dì shí sān zhāng

宠 辱 若 惊, 贵 大 患 若 身。
chǒng rǔ ruò jīng guì dà huàn ruò shēn

何 谓 宠 辱 若 惊? 宠 为 下, 得 之 若 惊, 失 之 若 惊,
hé wèi chǒng rǔ ruò jīng chǒng wéi xià dé zhī ruò jīng shī zhī ruò jīng

是 谓 宠 辱 若 惊。何 谓 贵 大 患 若 身?
shì wèi chǒng rǔ ruò jīng hé wèi guì dà huàn ruò shēn

吾 所 以 有 大 患 者, 为 吾 有 身, 及 吾 无 身, 吾 有 何 患?
wú suǒ yǐ yǒu dà huàn zhě wéi wú yǒu shēn jí wú wú shēn wú yǒu hé huàn

故 贵 以 身 为 天 下, 若 可 寄 天 下;
gù guì yǐ shēn wéi tiān xià ruò kě jì tiān xià

爱 以 身 为 天 下, 若 可 托 天 下。
ài yǐ shēn wéi tiān xià ruò kě tuō tiān xià

An ideal ruler should, first and foremost, value himself and refrain from acting wildly. Only a self-regarding man can cherish the lives of others and thus be entrusted with the task of ruling the state.

Honour and disgrace make no difference actually as far as the harm they do to our dignity is concerned. A man who is honoured always regards this as a special gift and hence tends to be worried about its loss. So, his dignity is also undermined.

Tao Te Ching
Chapter 14

Look at it yet it cannot be seen,
This is called "invisible".
Listen to it yet it cannot be heard,
This is called "silent".
Reach for it yet it cannot be touched,
This is called "intangible".
These three properties cannot be differentiated
Because they are mixed up as one.
Its upper part is not bright
And its lower part not dim.
Continuous and endless, it cannot be named,
And it returns to nothingness.
This is called the formless form
And the image of nothing;
This is also called the state of dimness.
Meet it without seeing its head,
Follow it without seeing its tail
Catch hold of the ancient Tao
To manage what is available now,
To know the origin of everything.
This is called the essence of Tao.

《道德经》第十四章
dào dé jīng dì shí sì zhāng

视之不见，名曰"夷"；听之不闻，名曰"希"；
shì zhī bú jiàn míng yuē yí   tīng zhī bù wén míng yuē xī

搏之不得，名曰"微"。
bó zhī bù dé míng yuē wēi

此三者不可致诘，故混而为一。
cǐ sān zhě bù kě zhì jié gù hùn ér wéi yī

其上不皦，其下不昧。绳绳兮不可名，复归于物。
qí shàng bù jiǎo qí xià bú wèi shéng shéng xī bù kě míng fù guī yú wù

是谓无状之状，无物之象，是谓惚恍。
shì wèi wú zhuàng zhī zhuàng wú wù zhī xiàng shì wèi huǎng hū

迎之不见其首；随之不见其后。
yíng zhī bú jiàn qí shǒu suí zhī bú jiàn qí hòu

执古之道，以御今之有。能知古始，是谓道纪。
zhí gǔ zhī dào yǐ yù jīn zhī yǒu néng zhī gǔ shǐ shì wèi dào jì

Shadowless and formless, Tao exists, transcending time and space and taking charge of everything in the world.

Tao Te Ching
Chapter 15

The ancients who knew Tao
Were of mysterious perception
And inexpressible profundity.
Because they were unfathomable,
They were portrayed in a fashion:
They were cautious like one crossing the river in winter,
Vigilant like one afraid of his neighbours,
Respectful like a guest,
Slack like ice about to thaw,
Simple like a piece of unprocessed wood,
Broad-minded like a valley,
And dim-witted like muddy water.
Muddy water, when staying still awhile,
Will become clear soon.
Still, when starting to move,
Will change step by step.
The follower of Tao does not seek fullness.
Because of this lack of fullness,
He can retain the old
And get the new at once.

《道德经》 第十五章
dào dé jīng dì shí wǔ zhāng

古 之 善 为 道 者，微 妙 玄 通，深 不 可 识。
gǔ zhī shàn wéi dào zhě wēi miào xuán tōng shēn bù kě shí

夫 唯 不 可 识，故 强 为 之 容：豫 兮 若 冬 涉 川；
fū wéi bù kě shí gù qiáng wéi zhī róng yù xī ruò dōng shè chuān

犹 兮 若 畏 四 邻；俨 兮 其 若 客；涣 兮 其 若 凌 释；
yóu xī ruò wèi sì líng yǎn xī qí ruò kè huàn xī qí ruò líng shì

敦 兮 其 若 朴；旷 兮 其 若 谷；混 兮 其 若 浊；
dūn xī qí ruò pǔ kuàng xī qí ruò gǔ hùn xī qí ruò zhuó

澹 兮 其 若 海；飂 兮 若 无 止。
dàn xī qí ruò hǎi liáo xī ruò wú zhǐ

孰 能 浊 以 静 之 徐 清；孰 能 安 以 动 之 徐 生。
shú néng zhuó yǐ jìng zhī xú qīng shú néng ān yǐ dòng zhī xú shēng

保 此 道 者，不 欲 盈。夫 唯 不 盈，故 能 蔽 而 新 成。
bǎo cǐ dào zhě bú yù yíng fū wéi bù yíng gù néng bì ér xīn chéng

Tao Te Ching
Chapter 16

Attain the ultimate emptiness,
Hold fast to a mind of peace.
The myriad things grow together,
And I watch them recycling.
Things are abundant,
They all return to their roots.
Such a return is to find peace,
To find peace is returning to life.
To return to life is to be constant,
Knowing the constant is to be illuminated.
Ignorance of it
Leads to wild acts.
Knowing brings tolerance,
Tolerance makes justice,
Justice results in kingly miens,
Kingly miens conforms to heavenly principle,
Heavenly principle complies with Tao.
Tao endures,
No danger comes in your life.

《道德经》 第十六章
dào dé jīng　dì shí liù zhāng

致 虚 极，守 静 笃。万 物 并 作，吾 以 观 复。
zhì xū jí　shǒu jìng dǔ　wàn wù bìng zuò　wú yǐ guān fù

夫 物 芸 芸，各 复 归 其 根。归 根 曰 静，静 曰 复 命。
fū wù yún yún　gè fù guī qí gēn　guī gēn yuē jìng　jìng yuē fù mìng

复 命 曰 常，知 常 曰 明。不 知 常，妄 作 凶。
fù mìng yuē cháng zhī cháng yuē míng bù zhī cháng wàng zuò xiōng

知 常 容，容 乃 公，公 乃 全，全 乃 天，
zhī cháng róng róng nǎi gōng gōng nǎi quán quán nǎi tiān

天 乃 道，道 乃 久，没 身 不 殆。
tiān nǎi dào　dào nǎi jiǔ　mò shēn bú dài

People should face the motion and evolution of the myriad things in the world with a serene and dispassionate mind. All things grow, die, revive and die again endlessly in compliance with their own laws.

Tao Te Ching
Chapter 17

As for the best ruler,
People do not know he exists.
As for the better ruler,
People come close to and praise him.
And as for a good ruler,
People hold him in awe.
When it comes to a bad ruler,
People despise him.
Lack of sincerity
Means popular trust is lost.
Just because he is of few words,
When things are accomplished,
The people say in unison:
We have acted naturally.

《道德经》第十七章
dào dé jīng dì shí qī zhāng

太上，不知有之；其次，亲而誉之；
tài shàng bù zhī yǒu zhī qí cì qīn ér yù zhī

其次，畏之；其次，侮之。信不足焉，有不信焉。
qí cì wèi zhī qí cì wǔ zhī xìn bù zú yān yǒu bú xìn yān

悠兮其贵言。功成事遂，百姓皆谓："我自然"。
yōu xī qí guì yán gōng chéng shì suì bǎi xìng jiē wèi wǒ zì rán

A good ruler should be sincere and honest. He should handle things in a relaxed and carefree manner and rarely issue orders. His government is nothing but an instrument for serving the people. Never should political power be imposed on the people.
In other words, people and their government should coexist on a peaceful basis, with each side acting in an appropriate and carefree way.

Tao Te Ching
Chapter 18

When the great Tao is discarded,
Humanity and justice appear.
When intellect is acquired,
Serious hypocrisy and deception come along.
When family members are in discord,
Filial piety and kindness emerge.
When the country is corrupt and unstable,
Loyal officials show up.

《道德经》 第十八章
dào dé jīng dì shí bā zhāng

大道废，有仁义；智慧出，有大伪；
dà dào fèi yǒu rén yì zhì huì chū yǒu dà wěi

六亲不和，有孝慈；国家昏乱，有忠臣。
liù qīn bù hé yǒu xiào cí guó jiā hūn luàn yǒu zhōng chén

Loyalty and filial piety are not highlighted when a country is well ruled and families are in harmony. Such good moral qualities are promoted only when a society needs them badly.

Tao Te Ching
Chapter 19

With holiness and wisdom abandoned,
The people will benefit a hundred-fold.
With humanity and justice rejected,
The people will revert to filial piety and compassion.
With guiles and interests discarded,
Thieves and burglars will disappear.
The above three,
Being not sufficient as rules,
Require strict adherence.
Exhibit plainness and keep to simplicity,
Reduce selfishness and minimise desire.
No learning, no worries.

《道德经》 第十九章
dào dé jīng   dì shí jiǔ zhāng

绝 圣 弃 智，民 利 百 倍；绝 仁 弃 义，民 复 孝 慈；
jué shèng qì zhì   mín lì bǎi bèi jué rén qì yì   mín fù xiào cí

绝 巧 弃 利，盗 贼 无 有。此 三 者 以 为 文，不 足。
jué qiǎo qì lì   dào zéi wú yǒu cǐ sān zhě yǐ wéi wén bù zú

故 令 有 所 属：见 素 抱 朴，少 私 寡 欲，绝 学 无 忧。
gù lìng yǒu suǒ shǔ jiàn sù bào pǔ shǎo sī guǎ yù   jué xué wú yōu

Tao Te Ching
Chapter 20

Yes and no,
What is the difference?
Good and evil,
How to distinguish between them?
What terrifies others
Also elicit fear in me.
Look afar and there is no end.
The people look very happy,
As if attending a sumptuous banquet,
Or enjoying beautiful spring on a platform.
Only I remain calm and unresponsive,
Like an infant not knowing how to smile,
Or like a low-spirited homeless man.
Everybody enjoys abundance,
While I alone suffer from scarcity.
I have a fool's mind,
Confused and obtuse.
Average people are enlightened,
While I alone remain muddle-headed.
The people are clear-minded,
While I alone remain confused.
All people have achieved something,
While I alone remain ignorant and stubborn.
The difference between others and me:
I value the nourishments of the mother.

《道 德 经》 第 二 十 章
dào dé jīng dì èr shí zhāng

唯 之 与 阿, 相 去 几 何? 美 之 与 恶, 相 去 若 何?
wéi zhī yú ā xiāng qù jǐ hé měi zhī yú è xiāng qù ruò hé

人 之 所 畏, 不 可 不 畏。 荒 兮, 其 未 央 哉!
rén zhī suǒ wèi bù kě bú wèi huāng xī qí wèi yāng zāi

众 人 熙 熙, 如 享 太 牢, 如 春 登 台。 我 独 泊 兮, 其 未 兆;
zhòng rén xī xī rú xiǎng tài láo rú chūn dēng tái wǒ dú bó xī qí wèi zhào

沌 沌 兮, 如 婴 儿 之 未 孩; 累 累 兮, 若 无 所 归。
dùn dùn xī rú yīn ér zhī wèi hái lěi lěi xī ruò wú suǒ guī

众 人 皆 有 余, 而 我 独 若 遗。 我 愚 人 之 心 也 哉!
zhòng rén jiē yǒu yú ér wǒ dú ruò yí wǒ yú rén zhī xīn yě zāi

俗 人 昭 昭, 我 独 昏 昏。 俗 人 察 察, 我 独 闷 闷。
sú rén zhāo zhāo wǒ dú hūn hūn sú rén chá chá wǒ dú mèn mèn

众 人 皆 有 以, 而 我 独 顽 且 鄙。 我 独 异 于 人, 而 贵 食 母。
zhòng rén jiē yǒu yǐ ér wǒ dú wán qiě bǐ wǒ dú yì yú rén ér guì shí mǔ

I am different from others. I worship the mother of everything in the world — the all-important Tao.

53

Tao Te Ching
Chapter 21

Acts of great virtue
Conform entirely to Tao.
The thing called "Tao"
Is misty and hazy.
Misty and hazy,
An image is visible there.
Hazy and misty,
Something material is there.
Obscure and dim,
A spirit is lurking there.
The spirit is real,
And also reliable.
From antiquity until today,
Its name has remained unchanged.
And in it can be seen the origin of
everything.
How do I know the origin of
everything as it is?
None other than this.

《道德经》第二十一章
dào dé jīng dì èr shí yī zhāng

孔德之容，惟道是从。道之为物，惟恍惟惚。
kǒng dé zhī róng wéi dào shì cóng dào zhī wéi wù wéi huǎng wéi hū

惚兮恍兮，其中有象；恍兮惚兮，其中有物。
hū xī huǎng xī qí zhōng yǒu xiàng huǎng xī hū xī qí zhōng yǒu wù

窈兮冥兮，其中有精；其精甚真，其中有信。
yǎo xī míng xī qí zhōng yǒu jīng qí jīng shèn zhēn qí zhōng yǒu xìn

自今及古，其名不去，以阅众甫。
zì jīn jí gǔ qí míng bú qù yǐ yuè zhòng fǔ

吾何以知众甫之状哉！以此。
wú hé yǐ zhī zhòng fǔ zhī zhuàng zāi yǐ cǐ

Invisible and formless, Tao is there indeed. Everything grows out of it. Virtue derives from it. Tao functions in a visible form called "Virtue".

Tao Te Ching Chapter 22

Compromise can lead to fulfilment,
Tortuous can become straight,
A low and empty place can be filled,
Old can become new,
Getting less also means getting more,
Avarice makes confusion.
Therefore, the sage observes the world's fortune with Tao,
Not ostentatious, he becomes self-conscious,
Not self-important, he becomes well known,
Not boastful, he becomes accomplished,
Not self-conceited, he becomes a leader.
Because he does not contend,
None can contend with him.
The ancient saying: "Compromise can lead to fulfilment,"
How can it be an empty talk?
Indeed fulfilment owes itself to Tao.

《道德经》 第二十二章
dào dé jīng dì èr shí èr zhāng

曲 则 全，枉 则 直，洼 则 盈，
qǔ zé quán wāng zé zhí wā zé yíng

敝 则 新，少 则 得，多 则 惑。
bì zé xīn shǎo zé dé duō zé huò

是 以 圣 人 抱 一 为 天 下 式。
shì yǐ shèng rén bào yī wéi tiān xià shì

不 自 见，故 明；不 自 是，故 彰；
bú zì xiàn gù míng bú zì shì gù zhāng

不 自 伐，故 有 功；不 自 矜，故 长。
bú zì fá gù yǒu gōng bú zì jīn gù cháng

夫 唯 不 争，故 天 下 莫 能 与 之 争。
fū wéi bù zhēng gù tiān xià mò néng yǔ zhī zhēng

古 之 所 谓 "曲 则 全" 者，岂 虚 言 哉！
gǔ zhī suǒ wèi qǔ zé quán zhě qǐ xū yán zāi

诚 全 而 归 之。
chéng quán ér guī zhī

Unity of opposites is a universal principle. The two opposites are even interchangeable. To attain the final objective, we must first place ourselves in a delicate and humble position.

Tao Te Ching
Chapter 23

To speak less is natural.
A gale does not blow a whole morning,
A shower does not last a whole day.
What makes them so?
Heaven and Earth.
If Heaven and Earth cannot have them last long,
Let alone men.
Therefore, people who follow Tao,
Are united with Tao;
People who follow Virtue are united with Virtue;
And people wanting Tao and Virtue go amiss.
Those who are united with Tao,
Are readily accepted by Tao.
Those who are united with Virtue
Are readily accepted by Virtue.
Those who have lost Tao and Virtue
Will also be forsaken by them.
No sufficient credit
Means no popular trust.

《道德经》第二十三章

dào dé jīng dì èr shí sān zhāng

希言自然。故飘风不终朝，骤雨不终日。

xī yán zì rán　gù piāo fēng bù zhōng zhāo zhòu yǔ bù zhōng rì

孰为此者? 天地。天地尚不能久，而况于人乎?

shú wéi cǐ zhě tiān dì　tiān dì shàng bù néng jiǔ　ér kuàng yú rén hū

故从事于道者，同于道；德者，同于德；失者，同于失。

gù cóng shì yú dào zhě tóng yú dào　dé zhě tóng yú dé　shī zhě tóng yú shī

同于道者，道亦乐得之；同于德者，德亦乐得之；

tóng yú dào zhě dào yì lè dé zhī tóng yú dé zhě dé yì lè dé zhī

同于失者，失亦乐得之。信不足焉，有不信焉。

tóng yú shī zhě shī yì lè dé zhī xìn bù zú yān yǒu bú xìn yān

Tao Te Ching
Chapter 24

Standing on tiptoe, you cannot keep balance.
Striding forward, you cannot go far.
If you are ostentatious you will not be self-conscious;
If you are self-important you will not become well known;
If you are boastful you will not become accomplished;
If you are self-conceited you will not shine.
Measured against Tao,
These acts are leftovers and warts,
Disgusting to people,
And a man who knows Tao will not commit such acts.

《道德经》 第二十四章
dào dé jīng　dì èr shí sì zhāng

企 者 不 立 ； 跨 者 不 行 ；
qǐ zhě bú lì　kuà zhě bù xíng

自 见 者 不 明 ； 自 是 者 不 彰 ；
zì jiàn zhě bù míng　zì shì zhě bù zhāng

自 伐 者 无 功 ； 自 矜 者 不 长 。
zì fá zhě wú gōng　zì jīn zhě bù zhǎng

其 在 道 也 ， 曰 ： 余 食 赘 形 。
qí zài dào yě　yuē　yú shí zhuì xíng

物 或 恶 之 ， 故 有 道 者 不 处 。
wù huò wù zhī　gù yǒu dào zhě bú chù

Tao Te Ching
Chapter 25

Something is made from mixing things.
It was born before Heaven and Earth.
Silent and empty,
Standing on its own, refusing to change,
Engaged in a never-ending cyclical motion,
It can be deemed the Mother of everything.
Not knowing its name,
I describe it as "Tao",
And name it "the Great" in a fashion.
It is great and endless,
Endless and distant,
Distant and returning.
Thus, Tao is great,
Heaven is great,
Earth is great,
And man is great.
There are four great things in the universe,
And man is one of them.
Man emulates Earth,
Earth emulates Heaven,
Heaven emulates Tao
And Tao emulates Nature.

《道德经》第二十五章
dào dé jīng dì èr shí wǔ zhāng

有物混成，先天地生。寂兮寥兮，
yǒu wù hùn chéng xiān tiān dì shēng jì xī liáo xī

独立而不改，周行而不殆，可以为天地母。
dú lì ér bù gǎi zhōu xíng ér bú dài kě yǐ wéi tiān dì mǔ

吾不知其名，强字之曰道，强为之名曰大。
wú bù zhī qí míng qiáng zì zhī yuē dào qiáng wéi zhī míng yuē dà

大曰逝，逝曰远，远曰反。
dà yuē shì shì yuē yuǎn yuǎn yuē fǎn

故道大，天大，地大，人亦大。
gù dào dà tiān dà dì dà rén yì dà

域中有四大，而人居其一焉。
yù zhōng yǒu sì dà ér rén jū qí yī yān

人法地，地法天，天法道，道法自然。
rén fǎ dì dì fǎ tiān tiān fǎ dào dào fǎ zì rán

Tao creates everything with no motive, allowing them to evolve by themselves. Tao is all-inclusive, crossing time and space, and rallies around itself everything in the world.

63

Tao Te Ching
Chapter 26

Heaviness is the root of lightness.
Equanimity is the ruler of restlessness.
Therefore the sage travels all day,
Without leaving behind his luggage.
Living in a grand palace,
He can still maintain an easy and detached life.
Why does a ruler with thousands of vehicles,
Rule the state in a frivolous and restless manner?
Frivolous, he will lose his root;
And restless, he will lose his sovereignty.

《道德经》第二十六章

dào dé jīng dì èr shí liù zhāng

重 为 轻 根，静 为 躁 君。

zhòng wéi qīng gēn jìng wéi zào jūn

是 以 君 子 终 日 行 不 离 辎 重。

shì yǐ jūn zǐ zhōng rì xíng bù lí zī zhòng

虽 有 荣 观，燕 处 超 然。

suī yǒu róng guān yàn chǔ chāo rán

奈 何 万 乘 之 主，而 以 身 轻 天 下?

nài hé wàn shèng zhī zhǔ ér yǐ shēn qīng tiān xià

轻 则 失 根，躁 则 失 君。

qīng zé shī gēn zào zé shī jūn

How can a king with thousands of vehicles ignore state affairs and indulge himself in personal pleasures? If he does not take seriously the state, he will lose the foundation of his administration. If he handles things in a restless manner, he will lose his sovereignty.

Tao Te Ching
Chapter 27

A good traveller leaves no tracks.
A good speaker leaves no accusable faults.
A good calculator needs no counting rods.
A latchless door, if well shut, cannot be opened.
A good knot, made not with rope, cannot be unravelled easily.
Therefore, the sage is ready to help people,
Rather than let them alone.
He is ready to rescue things,
Instead of discarding them.
This is called "comprehension of Tao".
Therefore, a good man
Is the teacher of a bad man;
And a bad man
Is the capital of a good man.
If the teacher is neglected,
And the capital is ignored,
An intelligent man can be an idiot,
This is called the secret principle.

《道德经》第二十七章
dào dé jīng dì èr shí qī zhāng

善行无辙迹，善言无瑕谪；善数不用筹策；
shàn xíng wú zhé jī shàn yán wú xiá zhé shàn shù bú yòng chóu cè

善闭无关楗而不可开，善结无绳约而不可解。
shàn bì wú guān jiàn ér bù kě kāi shàn jié wú shéng yuē ér bù kě jiě

是以圣人常善救人，故无弃人；
shì yǐ shèng rén cháng shàn jiù rén gù wú qì rén

常善救物，故无弃物。是谓袭明。
cháng shàn jiù wù gù wú qì wù shì wèi xí míng

故善人者，不善人之师；不善人者，善人之资。
gù shàn rén zhě bú shàn rén zhī shī bú shàn rén zhě shàn rén zhī zī

不贵其师，不爱其资，虽智大迷，是谓要妙。
bú guì qí shī bú ài qí zī suī zhì dà mí shì wèi yào miào

67

Tao Te Ching
Chapter 28

Know the masculine,
Yet hold on to the feminine,
Be a valley for everyone.
As the valley for everyone,
You'll have Virtue forever,
And return to infancy.
Know the white,
Yet hold on to the black,
Be a model for everyone.
As the model for everyone,
You will never lose Virtue or make any mistakes,
And you will return to the infinite.
Know honour,
Yet cling to disgrace,
Be a dale for everyone.
As the dale for everyone,
You'll have no end of virtue,
And also return to the simplicity of wood.
The wood becomes implements when cut,
Using them, the sage
Becomes a ruler.
Therefore, a great government needs no
cutting.

《道德经》第二十八章
dào dé jīng dì èr shí bā zhāng

知其雄，守其雌，为天下溪。
zhī qí xióng shǒu qí cí wéi tiān xià xī

为天下溪，常德不离，复归于婴儿。
wéi tiān xià xī cháng dé bù lí fù guī yú yīng ér

知其白，守其黑，为天下式。为天下式，
zhī qí bái shǒu qí hēi wéi tiān xià shì wéi tiān xià shì

常德不忒，复归于无极。知其荣，守其辱，为天下谷。
cháng dé bú tè fù guī yú wú jí zhī qí róng shǒu qí rǔ wéi tiān xià gǔ

为天下谷，常德乃足，复归于朴。
wéi tiān xià gǔ cháng dé nǎi zú fù guī yú pǔ

When confronted with social instability and disorder, we should adhere to the principle of "being feminine" so that we can go back to the truth and simplicity and bring about a perfect government.

Tao Te Ching
Chapter 29

If you want to get the world and rule it arbitrarily,
I don't think you will make it.
The world is a holy thing,
And it cannot be run arbitrarily.
Running it arbitrarily, you will fail,
Controlling it arbitrarily, you will lose it.
Thus the sage does not overdo, so he does not fail,
And the sage is not possessive, so he does not lose.
Therefore, some things lead and others follow,
Some breathe warm and others blow cool,
Some are strong and others weak,
Some protect and others destroy.
Therefore, the sage prevents extremism,
Shuns luxuriousness,
And avoids immoderacy.

《道德经》第二十九章
dào dé jīng   dì èr shí jiǔ zhāng

将 欲 取 天 下 而 为 之 , 吾 见 其 不 得 已 。
jiāng yù qǔ tiān xià ér wéi zhī   wú jiàn qí bù dé yǐ

天 下 神 器 , 不 可 为 也 , 不 可 执 也 。
tiān xià shén qì   bù kě wéi yě   bù kě zhí yě

为 者 败 之 , 执 者 失 之 。
wéi zhě bài zhī   zhí zhě shī zhī

是 以 圣 人 无 为 , 故 无 败 ; 无 执 , 故 无 失 。
shì yǐ shèng rén wú wéi   gù wú bài   wú zhí   gù wú shī

夫 物 或 行 或 随 ; 或 嘘 或 吹 ; 或 强 或 羸 ; 或 载 或 隳 。
fū wù huò xíng huò suí   huò xū huò chuī   huò qiáng huò léi   huò zāi huò huī

是 以 圣 人 去 甚 , 去 奢 , 去 泰 。
shì yǐ shèng rén qù shèn   qù shē   qù tài

Everything and everybody in the world have distinct individual characteristics. You are not expected to impose your own will on others. An ideal ruler is always able to abandon coercion, and follow Nature, guiding his actions in the light of circumstances and objective laws.

Tao Te Ching
Chapter 30

If you assist the king with Tao,
You will not resort to force of arms.
Military action would fire back in the end.
Where the army has camped,
Thorns and brambles grow wild.
At the heels of a war
Comes a year of famine.
Therefore, a good commander seeks only the end,
And never flaunts his military strength.
Victorious, he does not puff up,
Or become conceited,
Or become arrogant.
He deems the victory inevitable,
And never flaunts his superiority.
Things start to age when they are strong,
This is called a violation of Tao.
Premature death befalls things that go against Tao.

《道德经》 第三十章
dào dé jīng dì sān shí zhāng

以 道 佐 人 主 者，不 以 兵 强 天 下。
yǐ dào zuǒ rén zhǔ zhě bù yǐ bīng qiáng tiān xià

其 事 好 还。师 之 所 处，荆 棘 生 焉。
qí shì hǎo huán shī zhī suǒ chù jīng jí shēng yān

大 军 之 后，必 有 凶 年。
dà jūn zhī hòu bì yǒu xiōng nián

善 有 果 而 已，不 敢 以 取 强。
shàn yǒu guǒ ér yǐ bù gǎn yǐ qǔ qiáng

果 而 勿 矜，果 而 勿 伐，果 而 勿 骄。
guǒ ér wù jīn guǒ ér wù fá guǒ ér wù jiāo

果 而 不 得 已，果 而 勿 强。
guǒ ér bù dé yǐ guǒ ér wù qiáng

物 壮 则 老，是 谓 不 道，不 道 早 已。
wù zhuàng zé lǎo shì wèi bú dào bú dào zǎo yǐ

Tao Te Ching
Chapter 31

Weapons are ominous,
And nobody likes them.
Therefore they have no use for a man of Tao.
In daily life a gentleman values the left side,
And in military affairs the right side comes first.
Weapons are inauspicious,
And not intended for a gentleman.
Even when he has to use them,
He does not take them seriously.
Victory thus won is not to be applauded,
If applauded,
The victor enjoys killing.
A man who enjoys killing,
Will see his ambition of ruling a country
dashed.
The left is the place of honour on auspicious
occasions,
While the right is highly valued in an
inauspicious case.
The junior commander stands on the left.
And the senior commander on the right.
They are dealing with a war like a funeral.
As the war involves high casualties,
People go into a battle with a sad heart.
The victors handle it like a funeral.

《道德经》 第三十一章
dào dé jīng dì sān shí yī zhāng

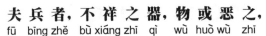

夫 兵 者，不 祥 之 器，物 或 恶 之，
fū bīng zhě bù xiáng zhī qì wù huò wù zhī

故 有 道 者 不 处。
gù yǒu dào zhě bù chǔ

君 子 居 则 贵 左，用 兵 则 贵 右。
jūn zi jū zé guì zuǒ yòng bīng zé guì yòu

兵 者 不 祥 之 器，非 君 子 之 器，
bīng zhě bù xiáng zhī qì fēi jūn zi zhī qì

不 得 已 而 用 之，恬 淡 为 上。
bù dé yǐ ér yòng zhī tián dàn wéi shàng

胜 而 不 美，而 美 之 者，是 乐 杀 人。
shèng ér bù měi ér měi zhī zhě shì lè shā rén

夫 乐 杀 人 者，则 不 可 得 志 于 天 下 矣。
fū lè shā rén zhě zé bù kě dé zhì yú tiān xià yi

吉 事 尚 左，凶 事 尚 右。
jí shì shàng zuǒ xiōng shì shàng yòu

偏 将 军 居 左，上 将 军 居 右，言 以 丧 礼 处 之。
piān jiāng jūn jū zuǒ shàng jiāng jūn jū yòu yán yi sàng li chǔ zhī

杀 人 之 众，以 悲 哀 泣 之，战 胜 以 丧 礼 处 之。
shā rén zhī zhòng yi bēi āi qì zhī zhàn shèng yǐ sàng li chǔ zhī

A war of arms is an inauspicious thing. A gentleman also needs a war to achieve his objective when no other option exists. However, he must bear in mind that he should not flaunt his power or kill indiscriminately.

Tao Te Ching
Chapter 32

Tao is eternal,
Though it is nameless and unvarnished.
Insignificant as it looks,
Nothing in the world can subjugate it.
If princes follow it,
Everything in the world will succumb to them.
When Heaven and Earth are married,
Sweet dew will fall.
Under no external order,
It is dispersed evenly on earth.
Things are created and names given,
With names given,
Heaven knows when to stop,
And keep away from perils.
The relationship of Tao and the world
Is like that of valley streams and rivers and seas.

《道德经》 第三十二章
dào dé jīng   dì sān shí èr zhāng

道 常 无 名、朴。虽 小，天 下 莫 能 臣。
dào cháng wú míng pǔ suī xiǎo tiān xià mò néng chén

侯 王 若 能 守 之，万 物 将 自 宾。
hóu wáng ruò néng shǒu zhī wàn wù jiāng zì bīn

天 地 相 合，以 降 甘 露，民 莫 之 令 而 自 均。
tiān dì xiāng hé yǐ jiàng gān lù mín mò zhī lìng ér zì jūn

始 制 有 名，名 亦 既 有，夫 亦 将 知 止，知 止 可 以 不 殆。
shǐ zhì yǒu míng míng yì jì yǒu fū yì jiāng zhī zhǐ zhī zhǐ kě yǐ bú dài

譬 道 之 在 天 下，犹 川 谷 之 于 江 海。
pì dào zhǐ zài tiān xià yóu chuān gǔ zhǐ yú jiāng hǎi

If a prince rules his country in accordance with the principles of Tao and in compliance with Nature, the people will subject themselves to his leadership.

Name is the root cause of all social conflicts. Therefore, you should know when and where to stop in instituting a system and defining names and positions. This is the only way to steer clear of troubles.

Tao Te Ching
Chapter 33

You are clever if you understand others,
You are wise if you know yourself.
You are strong if you overcome others,
You are great if you overcome yourself.
You are rich if you know how to be self-content,
you are ambitious if you work hard persistently.
You will prevail if you keep to nature,
you will live long if you do not depart after death.

《道德经》 第三十三章
dào dé jīng　　dì sān shí sān zhāng

知人者智，自知者明。
zhī rén zhě zhì　zì zhī zhě míng

胜人者有力，自胜者强。
shèng rén zhǒ yǒu lì　zì shèng zhě qiáng

知足者富。强行者有志。
zhī zú zhě fù　qiáng xíng zhě yǒu zhì

不失其所者久。死而不亡者寿。
bù shī qí suǒ zhě jiǔ　sǐ ér bù wáng zhě shòu

A man should cultivate a spiritually prosperous life. Knowing others and overcoming others are important. However, it is more important to know and overcome yourself. If you can examine yourself from time to time and stick to your own convictions by earnestly putting them into practice, you will have an energetic and ample life, both physically and spiritually.

Tao Te Ching
Chapter 34

Tao is a vast river,
It can run both left and right.
The myriad things live on it without being declined.
It accomplishes a lot but never seeks fame and ownership.
It nourishes everything but never lords over them.
It may be deemed small.
Everything returns to it but is not subjected to it,
And it may thus be deemed great.
Therefore, while never regarding himself great,
The sage is able to cultivate his greatness.

《道德经》 第三十四章
dào dé jīng dì sān shí sì zhāng

大道氾兮，其可左右。
dà dào fàn xī　 qí kě zuǒ yòu

万物恃之以生而不辞，功成而不有。
wàn wù shì zhī yǐ shēng ér bù cí　 gōng chéng ér bù yǒu

衣养万物而不为主，常无欲，可名于小；
yì yǎng wàn wù ér bù wéi zhǔ cháng wú yù　 kě míng yú xiǎo

万物归焉而不为主，可名为大。
wàn wù guī yān ér bù wéi zhǔ kě míng wéi dà

以其终不自为大，故能成其大。
yǐ qí zhōng bù zì wéi dà　 gù néng chéng qí dà

Tao Te Ching
Chapter 35

Grasping the Great Image,
The world will surrender itself.
With the world surrendered yet unharmed,
Peace and stability will ensue.
For music and delicacies,
Passersby stop.
Tao, when uttered,
Tastes bland and dull.
It is not pleasant when you look at it,
It is not sweet when you listen to it,
Yet it is inexhaustible when you use it.

《道德经》第三十五章
dào dé jīng   dì sān shí wǔ zhāng

执大象，天下往。往而不害，安平泰。
zhí dà xiàng tiān xià wǎng wǎng ér bú hài ān píng tài

乐与饵，过客止。
yuè yú ěr guò kè zhǐ

道之出口，淡乎其无味，
dào zhī chū kǒu dàn hū qí wú wèi

视之不足见，听之不足闻，用之不足既。
shì zhī bù zú jiàn tīng zhī bù zú wén yòng zhī bù zú jì

Tao is nothing extraordinary and attractive to many of us, but it plays an important role.

Tao Te Ching
Chapter 36

To contract something,
You must first expand it.
To weaken something,
You must first strengthen it.
To eliminate something,
You must first elevate it.
To take something,
You must first give.
This is a subtle stratagem:
The weak can outdo the strong.
Fish cannot stay away from ponds.
And sharp weapons of a country cannot
be brandished before the people.

《道德经》 第三十六章
dào dé jīng　　dì sān shí liù zhāng

将 欲 歙 之，必 固 张 之；将 欲 弱 之，必 固 强 之；
jiāng yù xī zhī　bì gù zhāng zhī　jiāng yù ruò zhī　bì gù qiáng zhī

将 欲 废 之，必 固 兴 之；将 欲 取 之，必 固 与 之。
jiāng yù fèi zhī　bì gù xīng zhī　jiāng yù qǔ zhī　bì gù yǔ zhī

是 谓 微 明。柔 弱 胜 刚 强。
shì wèi wēi míng　róu ruò shèng gāng qiáng

鱼 不 可 脱 于 渊，国 之 利 器 不 可 以 示 人
yú bù kě tuō yú yuān　guó zhī lì qì bù kě yǐ shì rén

Everything has two opposing sides. When one side develops to the fullest, the other side will rise and take its place. "No extreme will hold long" and "Nothing stays strong forever" are two aphorisms indicating the law governing the evolution of Nature. Therefore, rulers should not flaunt their power. They will not last long and even toll the death knell for themselves as long as they seek power through violence.

Tao Te Ching
Chapter 37

The eternal Tao does not exert itself
Yet it is capable of doing everything.
If princes can hold on to it,
The myriad things will evolve by themselves.
Evolving and rising,
They are restrained by simplicity.
Thus restrained,
They become desireless.
Desireless and tranquil,
The world becomes stable.

《道德经》 第三十七章
dào dé jīng　dì sān shí qī zhāng

道常无为而无不为。
dào cháng wú wéi ér wú bù wéi

侯王若能守之，万物将自化。
hóu wáng ruò néng shǒu zhī wàn wù jiāng zì huà

化而欲作，吾将镇之以无名之朴。
huà ér yù zuò　wú jiāng zhèn zhī yǐ wú míng zhī pǔ

镇之以无名之朴，夫将不欲。
zhèn zhī yǐ wú míng zhī pǔ　fū jiāng bú yù

不欲以静，天下将自正。
bú yù yǐ jìng　tiān xià jiāng zì zhèng

87

Tao Te Ching
Chapter 38

Higher virtue is amoral
And therefore it is virtuous.
Lower virtue is moral,
And thus it is non-virtuous.
Higher virtue is non-interfering and non-motivated,
Lower virtue is interfering and motivated.
Higher benevolence is interfering yet non-motivated,
Higher justice is interfering and motivated,
And higher propriety, interfering
And not appealing to people,
Is imposed by hand.
Therefore, Tao is lost and Virtue brought in,
Virtue lost and benevolence brought in,
Benevolence lost and justice brought in,
Justice lost and propriety brought in.
The so-called propriety,
Not supported by loyalty and sincerity,
Is the root cause of chaos.
The so-called "prescient"
Are merely flowers of Tao, heralding foolishness.
Therefore, the great man resides in the thick,
And keeps away from the thin.
Dwells in the substantial,
And steers clear of the superficial,
He takes this while giving up that.

《道 德 经》 第 三 十 八 章
dào dé jīng dì sān shí bā zhāng

上 德 不 德，是 以 有 德；下 德 不 失 德，是 以 无 德。
shàng dé bù dé shì yǐ yǒu dé   xià dé bù shī dé shì yǐ wú dé

上 德 无 为 而 无 以 为；下 德 无 为 而 有 以 为。
shàng dé wú wéi ér wú yǐ wéi   xià dé wú wéi ér yǒu yǐ wéi

上 仁 为 之 而 无 以 为；上 义 为 之 而 有 以 为。
shàng rén wéi zhī ér wú yǐ wéi   shàng yì wéi zhī ér yǒu yǐ wéi

上 礼 为 之 而 莫 之 应，则 攘 臂 而 扔 之。
shàng lǐ wéi zhī ér mò zhī yìng zé rǎng bì ér rēng zhī

故 失 道 而 后 德，失 德 而 后 仁，
gù shī dào ér hòu dé shī dé ér hòu rén

失 仁 而 后 义，失 义 而 后 礼。
shī rén ér hòu yì shī yì ér hòu lǐ

夫 礼 者，忠 信 之 薄，而 乱 之 首。
fū lǐ zhě zhōng xìn zhī bó ér luàn zhī shǒu

前 识 者，道 之 华，而 愚 之 始。
qián shí zhě dào zhī huá ér yú zhī shǐ

是 以 大 丈 夫 处 其 厚，不 居 其 薄；
shì yǐ dà zhàng fū chǔ qí hòu bù jū qí bó

处 其 实，不 居 其 华。故 去 彼 取 此。
chǔ qí shí bù jū qí huá gù qù bǐ qǔ cǐ

All ideas on promoting virtue, benevolence, justice and propriety are developed because of the loss of Tao in the world. Virtue, benevolence, justice and propriety are secondary when compared with Tao.

A society ruled by virtue, benevolence, justice and propriety is not an ideal one. A man should maintain his natural self, which is grounded in plainness and simplicity, in the midst of those who neglect mutual love and pursue the superficial and insubstantial.

Tao Te Ching
Chapter 39

These things from of old have acquired Oneness:
Heaven becomes clear,
Earth becomes stable,
Spirits become spiritual,
Valleys run in full
Everything lives on,
And princes become rulers of the world.
Let's deduce from here:
Without clarity, Heaven falls apart,
Without stability, Earth is destroyed,
Without spirituality, spirits have to rest.
Without fullness, valleys go dry,
Without life, everything in the world will perish,
And princes will be overthrown for dearth of nobleness.
Thus, the noble is based on the humble,
And the high is founded on the low.
Thus, princes consider themselves as the orphaned, the lonely and the unkind,
Is this an instance of being based on humbleness?
Isn't it?
Therefore, excessive applause means no praise,
And the sage would rather be as hard as rock
Than be as noble as jade.

《道德经》 第三十九章
dào dé jīng dì sān shí jiǔ zhāng

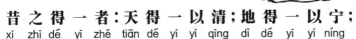

昔 之 得 一 者：天 得 一 以 清；地 得 一 以 宁；
xī zhī dé yī zhě tiān dé yī yǐ qīng dì dé yī yǐ níng

神 得 一 以 灵；谷 得 一 以 盈；
shén dé yī yǐ líng gǔ dé yī yǐ yíng

万 物 得 一 以 生；侯 王 得 一 以 为 天 下 正。
wàn wù dé yī yǐ shēng hóu wáng dé yī yǐ wéi tiān xià zhèng

其 致 之 也，谓 天 无 以 清，将 恐 裂；
qí zhì zhī yě wèi tiān wú yǐ qīng jiāng kǒng liè

地 无 以 宁，将 恐 废；神 无 以 灵，将 恐 歇；
dì wú yǐ níng jiāng kǒng fèi shén wú yǐ líng jiāng kǒng xiē

谷 无 以 盈，将 恐 竭；万 物 无 以 生，将 恐 灭；
gǔ wú yǐ yíng jiāng kǒng jié wàn wù wú yǐ shēng jiāng kǒng miè

侯 王 无 以 正，将 恐 蹶。
hóu wáng wú yǐ zhèng jiāng kǒng jué

故 贵 以 贱 为 本，高 以 下 为 基。
gù guì yǐ jiàn wéi běn gāo yǐ xià wéi jī

是 以 侯 王 自 称 孤、寡、不 谷。
shì yǐ hóu wáng zì chēng gū guǎ bù gǔ

此 非 以 贱 为 本 邪? 非 乎? 故 至 誉 无 誉。
cǐ fēi yǐ jiàn wéi běn yé fēi hū gù zhì yù wú yù

是 故 不 欲 琭 琭 如 玉，珞 珞 如 石。
shì gù bú yù lù lù rú yù luò luò rú shí

Tao is indispensable. Without it, everything will not survive.

All rulers must proceed from the principles of Tao and be willing to stay low, stand back and remain humble. Without the support of the masses, they will not become noble rulers.

Tao Te Ching
Chapter 40

Reversion is the movement of Tao,
And being soft is its function.
Everything in the universe is born of being,
And being is born of nothingness.

《道德经》第四十章
dào dé jīng dì sì shí zhāng

反者道之动；弱者道之用。
fǎn zhě dào zhī dòng ruò zhě dào zhī yòng

天下万物生于有，有生于无。
tiān xià wàn wù shēng yú yǒu yǒu shēng yú wú

Abide by the law of Tao, and allow everything to evolve on its own.

It is irrational to seek quick success and immediate benefits by arbitrary means.

Tao Te Ching
Chapter 41

When superior men hear of Tao,
They work hard to practise it.
When average men hear of Tao,
They regard it with suspicion.
When inferior men hear of Tao,
They deride it.
Tao cannot be so called unless derided,
Therefore an aphorism has it:
The bright path looks dark,
Advancing seems retreating,
And the flat path looks bumpy.
The high virtue is like a valley,
Vast virtue looks insufficient,
Healthy virtue seems ill,
Loyalty becomes betrayal,
Pure white is like black dirt,
Great square has no corner,
Precious things take time to be made,
Great sound is not audible,
Great image has no shape,
Tao is grand but nameless.
So, only Tao,
Begins well and ends perfect.

《道 德 经》 第 四 十 一 章
dào dé jīng   dì sì shí yī zhāng

上 士 闻 道，勤 而 行 之；中 士 闻 道，若 存 若 亡；
shàng shì wén dào qín ěr xíng zhī zhōng shì wén dào ruò cún ruò wáng

下 士 闻 道，大 笑 之。
xià shì wén dào dà xiào zhī

不 笑 不 足 以 为 道。故 建 言 有 之：
bú xiào bù zú yǐ wéi dào gù jiàn yán yǒu zhī

明 道 若 昧；进 道 若 退；夷 道 若 颣；
míng dào ruò mèi jìn dào ruò tuì yí dào ruò lèi

上 德 若 谷；广 德 若 不 足；建 德 若 偷；
shàng dé ruò gǔ guǎng dé ruò bù zú jiàn dé ruò tōu

质 真 若 渝；大 白 若 辱；大 方 无 隅；大 器 晚 成；
zhì zhēn ruò ùv dà bá ruò rǔ dà fāng wú yú dà qì wǎn chéng

大 音 希 声；大 象 无 形；道 隐 无 名。
dà yīn xī shēng dà xiàng wú xíng dào yǐn wú míng

夫 唯 道，善 贷 且 成。
fū wéi dào shàn dài qiě chéng

Subtle and abstruse, Tao is beyond the comprehension of ordinary people. Opposition and mutual dependence are the laws governing the development of everything in the world.

Tao Te Ching
Chapter 42

Tao creates one,
One creates two.
Two creates three,
And three creates everything in the world.
Things face the yang with its back to the yin,
And yin and yang combine to achieve harmony.

People hate terms like the
orphaned,
the lonely and the unkind.
Yet princes and dukes adopt
these titles.
Thus, things may gain from loss,
Or lose for what they gain.
What is taught by others,
I also teach:
"He who is arrogant and
domineering shall not end
up well."
I take this as the beginning
of my teaching.

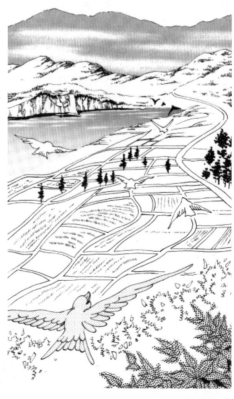

《道德经》第四十二章
dào dé jīng dì sì shí èr zhāng

道 生 一，一 生 二，二 生 三，三 生 万 物。
dào shēng yī yī shēng èr èr shēng sān sān shēng wàn wù

万 物 负 阴 而 抱 阳，冲 气 以 为 和。
wàn wù fù yīn ér bào yáng chōng qì yǐ wéi hé

人 之 所 恶，唯 孤、寡、不 谷，
rén zhī suǒ wù wéi gū guǎ bù gǔ

而 王 公 以 为 称。
ér wáng gōng yǐ wéi chēng

故 物 或 损 之 而 益，或 益 之 而 损。
gù wù huò sǔn zhī ér yì huò yì zhī ér sǔn

人 之 所 教，我 亦 教 之。
rén zhī suǒ jiāo wǒ yì jiāo zhī

强 梁 者 不 得 其 死，
qiáng liáng zhě bù dé qí sǐ

吾 将 以 为 教 父。
wú jiāng yǐ wéi jiào fù

Tao mixes up yin and yang when creating the myriad things in the world. Loss and gain as seen in the evolution of everything are caused by an imbalance between yin and yang.

Everything in the world develops in a dialectical and contradictory manner. The two opposing sides can also be united, and they are even inter-changeable.

Tao Te Ching
Chapter 43

The softest thing in the world
Is able to run in and out of the hardest thing.
The invisible can penetrate the densest,
Thus I know the benefit of inaction.
Teaching without words,
Gain without action,
Can hardly be achieved by anything in the world.

《道德经》 第四十三章
dào dé jīng　　dì sì shí sān zhāng

天 下 之 至 柔, 驰 骋 天 下 之 至 坚。
tiān xià zhī zhì róu　chí chéng tiān xià zhī zhì jiān

无 有 入 无 间, 吾 是 以 知 无 为 之 有 益。
wú yǒu rù wú jiān　wú shì yǐ zhī wú wéi zhī yǒu yì

不 言 之 教, 无 为 之 益, 天 下 希 及 之。
bù yán zhī jiào　wú wéi zhī yì　tiān xià xī jí zhī

Water dropping day by day wears the hardest rock away. The soft and weak can overcome the strong and powerful. Deep inside the softest and weakest thing is stored an immense power about which the strongest thing can do nothing.

Tao Te Ching
Chapter 44

Which is dearer, fame or life?
Which is more precious, life or possessions?
Which is more worrisome, gain or loss?
Extreme greed results in severe waste,
And excessive stock leads to grievous loss.
Thus, self-contentment does not incur humiliation,
Knowing the limits does not bring danger.
Only thus can you endure.

《道德经》 第四十四章

dào dé jīng　　dì sì shí sì zhāng

名 与 身 孰 亲? 身 与 货 孰 多? 得 与 亡 孰 病?

míng yú shēn shú qīn　　shēn yú huò shú duō　　dé yú wáng shú bìng

甚 爱 必 大 费;多 藏 必 厚 亡。

shèn ài bì dà fèi　　duō cáng bì hòu wáng

故 知 足 不 辱,知 止 不 殆,可 以 长 久。

gù zhī zú bù rǔ　　zhī zhǐ bú dài　　kě yǐ cháng jiǔ

Tao Te Ching
Chapter 45

Outstanding achievement seems imperfect,
Yet its function is not compromised.
Great fullness seems empty,
Yet its function is not limited.
Great straightness looks twisted,
Superior skills look clumsy,
Extraordinary eloquence looks close-lipped.
Jogging overcomes cold,
Quietude overcomes heat,
Peace is the ruler of the world.

《道德经》 第四十五章
dào dé jīng　　dì sì shí wǔ zhāng

大 成 若 缺，其 用 不 弊。
dà chéng ruò quē　qí yòng bú bì

大 盈 若 冲，其 用 不 穷。
dà yíng ruò chōng qí yòng bù qióng

大 直 若 屈，大 巧 若 拙，大 辩 若 讷。
dà zhí ruò qū　dà qiǎo ruò zhuō dà biàn ruò nè

静 胜 躁，寒 胜 热。清 静 为 天 下 正。
jìng shèng zào hán shèng rè qīng jìng wéi tiān xià zhèng

Tao Te Ching
Chapter 46

When Tao prevails in a country,
Steeds are used to pull dung-carts.
When Tao is discarded,
Ponies are born at the border.
No evil act is worse than an inordinate desire,
No disaster is worse than an insatiable demand,
And no mistake is worse than an unsatisfiable hunger.
Hence, only he who knows how to be satisfied,
Will remain satisfied forever.

《道德经》 第四十六章
dào dé jīng   dì sì shí liù zhāng

天 下 有 道，却 走 马 以 粪。
tiān xià yǒu dào què zǒu mǎ yǐ fèn

天 下 无 道，戎 马 生 于 郊。
tiān xià wú dào róng mǎ shēng yú jiāo

祸 莫 大 于 不 知 足；咎 莫 大 于 欲 得。
huò mò dà yú bù zhī zú jiù mò dà yú yù dé

故 知 足 之 足，常 足 矣。
gù zhī zú zhī zú cháng zú yǐ

Wars breakout between countries because rulers entertain strong desires. To cool down their desires, rulers should act on the principles of Tao. Only thus can the world be blessed with a millennium.

Tao Te Ching
Chapter 47

Know everything while staying indoors,
Identify the way of Heaven without looking through the window.
The further you go,
The less you know.
Hence, the sage knows without practice,
Understands without seeing,
And accomplishes without exertion.

《道德经》 第四十七章
dào dé jīng　　dì sì shí qī zhāng

不出户，知天下；不窥牖，见天道。
bù chū hù　zhī tiān xià　bù kuī yǒu　jiàn tiān dào

其出弥远，其知弥少。
qí chū mí yuǎn　qí zhī mí shǎo

是以圣人不行而知，不见而明，不为而成。
shì yǐ shèng rén bù xíng ér zhī　bú jiàn ér míng　bù wéi ér chéng

The more you investigate, the more closely you observe, the less you know.

Tao Te Ching
Chapter 48

In studying, progress is made every day.
In practising Tao, loss is incurred every day.
Loss upon loss,
Till non-action is attained,
Nothing is done yet everything is accomplished.
To rule the world non-intervention should be used,
When intervention takes place,
The world cannot be ruled well.

《道德经》 第四十八章
dào dé jīng　　dì sì shí bā zhāng

为 学 日 益，为 道 日 损。
wéi xué rì yì　wéi dào rì sǔn

损 之 又 损，以 至 于 无 为。
sǔn zhī yòu sǔn　yǐ zhì yú wú wéi

无 为 而 无 不 为。
wú wéi ér wú bù wéi

取 天 下 常 以 无 事，及 其 有 事，不 足 以 取 天 下。
qǔ tiān xià cháng yǐ wú shì　jí qí yǒu shì　bù zú yǐ qǔ tiān xià

Academic study aims at outward experience and knowledge. The more you accumulate, the more you become opinionated and prejudiced. In contrast, to practise Tao, you must get rid of personal desires and prejudices and go back to simplicity and truth.

Tao Te Ching
Chapter 49

The sage has no selfish mind,
He regards the people's mind as his own.
I treat the kind fairly,
I treat the unkind fairly too,
Thus kindness is acquired.
I trust the trustworthy,
I trust also those who are not trustworthy.
Thus trust is established.
The sage restrains his own desires as a ruler,
Helps people restore simplicity and modesty.
The people concentrate on what they see
and hear,
While the sage treats them as his children.

《道 德 经》 第 四 十 九 章
dào dé jīng dì sì shí jiǔ zhāng

圣 人 常 无 心 , 以 百 姓 心 为 心 。
shèng rén cháng wú xīn yǐ bǎi xìng xīn wéi xīn

善 者 , 吾 善 之 ; 不 善 者 , 吾 亦 善 之 ; 德 善 。
shàn zhě wú shàn zhī bú shàn zhě wú yì shàn zhī dé shàn

信 者 , 吾 信 之 ; 不 信 者 , 吾 亦 信 之 ; 德 信 。
xìn zhě wú xìn zhī bú xìn zhě wú yì xìn zhī dé xìn

圣 人 在 天 下 , 歙 歙 焉 , 为 天 下 浑 其 心 ,
shèng rén zài tiān xià xī xī yān wéi tiān xià hún qí xīn

百 姓 皆 注 其 耳 目 , 圣 人 皆 孩 之 。
bǎi xìng jiē zhù qí ěr mù shèng rén jiē hái zhī

Ruling the country by Tao, the sage is able to ensure that everybody returns to the innocent state of infanthood and enjoys a healthy and long life.

Tao Te Ching
Chapter 50

We are born and go back to death.
Three in ten live a long life,
Three in ten die young,
And three in ten die from indiscretion.
Why is this so?
Because they work so hard to live.
I hear a good health preserver
Does not shun rhinos and tigers in mountains,
Does not wear armours and knives on the battleground.
Rhinos cannot attack him with their horns,
Tigers cannot strike him with their claws,
And knives find no place in him for their blades.
Why is this so?
Because he belongs not to the realm of death.

《道 德 经》 第 五 十 章
dào dé jīng dì wǔ shí zhāng

出 生 入 死。生 之 徒，十 有 三；死 之 徒，十 有 三；
chū shēng rù sǐ shēng zhī tú shí yǒu sān sǐ zhī tú shí yǒu sān

人 之 生，动 之 于 死 地，亦 十 有 三。
rén zhī shēng dòng zhī yú sǐ dì yì shí yǒu sān

夫 何 故? 以 其 生 之 厚。
fū hé gù yǐ qí shēng zhī hòu

盖 闻 善 摄 生 者，陆 行 不 遇 兕 虎，入 军 不 被 甲 兵；
gài wén shàn shè shēng zhě lù xíng bú yù sì hǔ rù jūn bú bèi jiǎ bīng

兕 无 所 投 其 角，虎 无 所 用 其 爪，兵 无 所 容 其 刃。
sì wú suǒ tóu qí jiǎo hǔ wú suǒ yòng qí zhuǎ bīng wú suǒ róng qí rèn

夫 何 故? 以 其 无 死 地。
fū hé gù yǐ qí wú sǐ dì

Tao Te Ching
Chapter 51

Tao gives birth to everything,
Virtue raises it,
The matter shapes it,
And utilities materialise it.
Hence, Tao is widely respected and Virtue highly valued.
That Tao is respectable,
And Virtue is valuable,
Is spontaneous rather than forced.
Thus, Tao gives birth to everything,
Virtue raises it,
Promoting its growth.
Stimulating its maturity,
Nourishing and protecting it,
Giving birth to it not for possessing,
Acting yet not for ostentation,
Promoting its growth not for control.
This is the so-called mysterious and abstruse Virtue.

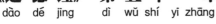

《道德经》 第五十一章
dào dé jīng　dì wǔ shí yī zhāng

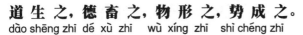

道 生 之, 德 畜 之, 物 形 之, 势 成 之。
dào shēng zhī dé xù zhī　wù xíng zhī　shì chéng zhī

是 以 万 物 莫 不 尊 道 而 贵 德。
shì yǐ wàn wù mò bù zūn dào ér guì dé

道 之 尊, 德 之 贵, 夫 莫 之 命 而 常 自 然。
dào zhī zūn　dé zhī guì　fū mò zhī mìng ér cháng zì rán

故 道 生 之, 德 畜 之;长 之 育 之;亭 之 毒 之;养 之 覆 之。
gù dào shēng zhī dé xù zhī zhǎng zhī yù zhī　tíng zhī dú zhī yǎng zhī fù zhī

生 而 不 有, 为 而 不 恃, 长 而 不 宰。是 谓 玄 德。
shēng ér bù yǒu　wéi ér bù shì zhǎng ér bù zǎi　shì wèi xuán dé

> Virtue is Tao incarnate and the concrete function of Tao in society.

Tao Te Ching
Chapter 52

Heaven and Earth have a beginning,
Which mothers everything in the world.
Knowing the mother,
We can know the children.
Knowing the children,
And clinging to the mother at once,
We can remain safe and sound till death.
Stop all holes,
Close all doors,
We will remain carefree lifelong.
Open all holes,
Let in everything,
We will become out of control.
Understanding the subtle is called enlightenment,
Remaining gentle and weak is called strength.
Using its light,
Also reverting to its source,
And incurring no disasters,
This is called complying with the eternal.

《道德经》第五十二章
dào dé jīng dì wǔ shí èr zhāng

天下有始，以为天下母。
tiān xià yǒu shǐ yǐ wéi tiān xià mǔ

既得其母，以知其子；
jì dé qí mǔ yǐ zhī qí zi

既知其子，复守其母，没身不殆。
jì dé qí zi fù shǒu qí mǔ mò shēn bú dài

塞其兑，闭其门，终身不勤。
sāi qí duì bì qí mén zhōng shēn bù qín

开其兑，济其事，终身不救。见小曰明，守柔曰强。
kāi qí duì jì qí shì zhōng shēn bú jiù jiàn xiǎo yuē míng shǒu róu yuē qiáng

用其光，复归其明，无遗身殃；是为袭常。
yòng qí guāng fù guī qí míng wú yí shēn yāng shì wéi xí cháng

> The development of everything in the world can be traced to a general origin. Pursue this origin and grasp it as a principle. Do not deviate from the origin when trying to know the world. Do not pursue things outside the origin. Otherwise, you will lose your identity.

Tao Te Ching
Chapter 53

If I possess a bit of knowledge,
I will walk along the Great Tao,
Lest I stray from it.
The Great Tao is flat,
Whereas people tend to take a winding path.
When the court is corrupt,
The farmland goes fallow
And the granaries become empty.
Dressed elegantly,
Wearing sharp swords,
Satiated with drink and food,
And having extra wealth,
This is what a ringleader is like.
And certainly this goes against Tao!

《道 德 经》 第 五 十 三 章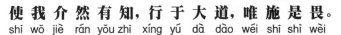
dào dé jīng　dì wǔ shí sān zhāng

使 我 介 然 有 知，行 于 大 道，唯 施 是 畏。
shǐ wǒ jiè rán yǒu zhī xíng yú dà dào wéi shī shì wèi

大 道 甚 夷，而 人 好 径。
dà dào shèn yí　ér rén hào jìng

朝 甚 除，田 甚 芜，仓 甚 虚；
cháo shèn chú tián shèn wú cāng shèn xū

服 文 彩，带 利 剑，厌 饮 食，财 货 有 余；
fú wén cǎi dài lì jiàn yàn yǐn shí cái huò yǒu yú

是 谓 盗 夸。非 道 也 哉！
shì wèi dào kuā fēi dào yě zāi

In a dark society, people live in great misery. The rulers abuse their power and tyrannise the people, pressing and exploiting them unscrupulously. As a result, most of the lower people live in hunger. Such acts are no different from robbery.

Tao Te Ching
Chapter 54

What is well constructed cannot be pulled down,
What is tightly held does not slip away,
Coming generations will worship their ancestors without end.
Cultivate virtue in yourself
You will get true virtue.
Cultivate it in the family
The family will overflow with virtue.
Cultivate it in the town
Virtue will be extended.
Cultivate it in the country
Virtue will be expanded.
Cultivate it in the world
Virtue will be widely accepted.
Thus, regard other individuals as yourself,
Regard other families as your own,
Regard other countries as your own,
Regard the future world as the present one,
This is also
Why I can know Tao of the world.

《道德经》 第五十四章
dào dé jīng　　　dì wǔ shí sì zhāng

善建者不拔，善抱者不脱，子孙以祭祀不辍。
shàn jiàn zhě bù bá shàn bào zhě bù tuō zi sūn yi jì sì bú chuò

修之于身，其德乃真；修之于家，其德乃余；
xiū zhī yú shēn qí dé nǎi zhēn xiū zhī yú jiā qí dé nǎi yú

修之于乡，其德乃长；修之于邦，其德乃丰；
xiū zhī yú xiāng qí dé nǎi cháng xiū zhī yú bāng qí dé nǎi fēng

修之于天下，其德乃普。
xiū zhī yú tiān xià qí dé nǎi pǔ

故以身观身，以家观家，以乡观乡，
gù yi shēn guān shēn yi jiā guān jiā yi xiāng guān xiāng

以邦观邦，以天下观天下。
yi bāng guān bāng yi tiān xià guān tiān xià

吾何以知天下然哉？以此。
wú hé yi zhī tiān xià rán zāi yi ci

The principle of personal cultivation is the foundation on which a person lives and conducts himself in this world. Only by consolidating this foundation can a person establish himself, and serve his family, his country and the world.

Tao Te Ching
Chapter 55

A man of great virtue
Is like a newborn child.
Hornets, scorpions and snakes do not sting it,
Fierce beasts do not attack it,
Hawks do not pounce on it.
Despite its fragile bones and soft muscles,
It can have a firm grip on things.
With no knowledge of copulation, its genitals are erect,
As a result of its sufficient vitality.
It cries all day long yet its voice remains clear and sharp,
As a result of its internal harmony.
Knowing harmony is called constancy,
Knowing constancy is called illumination,
Working hard to live is called disaster,
Vitality driven by desire is called presumptuousness.
Things start to age when they are strong,
This is called violation of Tao.
Premature death befalls things contrary to Tao.

《道德经》 第五十五章
dào dé jīng   dì wǔ shí wǔ zhāng

含 德 之 厚，比 于 赤 子。
hán dé zhī hòu bǐ yú chì zǐ

毒 虫 不 螫，猛 兽 不 据，攫 鸟 不 搏。
dú chóng bú shì měng shòu bù jū jué niǎo bù bó

骨 弱 筋 柔 而 握 固。未 知 牝 牡 之 合 而 朘 作，精 之 至 也。
gǔ ruò jīn róu ér wò gù wèi zhī pìn mǔ zhī hé ér juān zuò jīng zhī zhì yě

终 日 号 而 不 嗄，和 之 至 也。
zhōng rì háo ér bú shà hé zhī zhì yě

知 和 曰 "常"，知 常 曰 "明"。益 生 曰 祥。心 使 气 曰 强。
zhī hé yuē cháng zhī cháng yuē míng yì shēng yuē xiáng xīn shǐ qì yuē qiáng

物 壮 则 老，谓 之 不 道，不 道 早 已。
wù zhuàng zé lǎo wèi zhī bú dào bú dào zǎo yǐ

You will violate Tao when you abandon yourself to corporeal delight and flaunt your superiority. As a result, you will go through a decline from youth to senility and meet your death in the end.

123

Tao Te Ching
Chapter 56

A learned man is silent.
An ignorant man speaks loudly.
Stop all holes,
Close all doors,
Blunt sharpness,
Disentangle knots,
Soften glare,
And mix with earth.
This is what subtle oneness means.
You cannot acquire it, but you can befriend it,
Or be estranged from it.
You cannot acquire it, but it can benefit you,
Or bring harm to you.
You cannot acquire it, but it can make you noble,
Or make you contemptible.
Thus you can be held in esteem by the world.

《道德经》 第五十六章
dào dé jīng   dì wǔ shí liù zhāng

知者不言，言者不知。
zhī zhě bù yán yán zhě bù zhī

塞其兑，闭其门；挫其锐，解其纷，
sāi qí duì bì qí mén cuò qí ruì jiě qí fēn

和其光，同其尘，是谓"玄同"。
hé qí guāng tóng qí chén shì wèi xuán tóng

故不可得而亲，不可得而疏；
gù bù kě dé ér qīn bù kě dé ér shū

不可得而利，不可得而害；
bù kě dé ér lì bù kě dé ér hài

不可得而贵，不可得而贱。故为天下贵。
bù kě dé ér guì bù kě dé ér jiàn gù wéi tiān xià guì

The peak of human cultivation is to identify with Tao. To this end, a man should attach great importance to personal development, eliminate selfish thoughts, and refrain from showing off his talents.

We should take a detached attitude toward conflicts and blend ourselves with the mundane world. At the same time, we should not show special concern for intimacy and estrangement, gain and loss, nobleness and humbleness. We are expected to regard all people and things with a broad and impartial mind.

Tao Te Ching
Chapter 57

Govern the state by normal means,
Direct battles with surprising tactics.
Win the world through non-interference.
This is also
How I know Tao of the world.
The more regulations there are,
The poorer the people become;
The more sharp swords the king owns,
The more disorderly the state becomes.
The cleverer the people are,
The more evils there are.
The more laws are enacted,
The more thieves and outlaws there are.
Thus the sages say:
"I am not coercive, and the people become civilised themselves.
I delight in silence, and the people improve themselves.
I do not interfere, and the people get rich themselves.
I am not greedy, and the people
become natural and guileless."

《道德经》 第五十七章
dào dé jīng　　dì wǔ shí qī zhāng

以正治国，以奇用兵，以无事取天下。
yǐ zhèng zhì guó　yǐ qí yòng bīng　yǐ wú shì qǔ tiān xià

吾何以知其然哉? 以此：
wú hé yǐ zhī qí rán zāi　yǐ cǐ

天下多忌讳，而民弥贫；人多利器，国家滋昏；
tiān xià duō jì huì　ér mín mí pín　rén duō lì qì　guó jiā zī hūn

人多伎巧，奇物滋起；法令滋彰，盗贼多有。
rén duō jì qiǎo　qí wù zī qǐ　fǎ lìng zī zhāng dào zéi duō yǒu

故圣人："我无为，而民自化；我好静，而民自正；
gù shèng rén　wǒ wú wéi　ér mín zì huà　wǒ hào jìng　ér mín zì zhèng

我无事，而民自富；我无欲，而民自朴。"
wǒ wú shì　ér mín zì fù　wǒ wú yù　ér mín zì pǔ

Administrators tend to believe that they play a special role in the society and come up with all kinds of standards and norms based on their own understanding and impose them on the people. If all of them can adhere to the principles of "non-interference", "tranquillity" and "selflessness", it won't be long before we can have a stable and peaceful society.

Tao Te Ching
Chapter 58

When the administration is broad-minded,
The people become guileless.
When the government is strict and picky,
The people become cunning and crafty.
Misfortune contains fortune,
And fortune foretells misfortune.
Who knows their ultimate limits?
They cannot be defined by definite norms.
Justice may change to its opposite,
And goodness may revert to badness.
The people remain confused
For a long time.
Thus the sages square things without cutting.
Having sharp weapons, they do not hurt,
Being straightforward, they do not overstep,
Though bright, they do not blind.

《道 德 经》　第 五 十 八 章
dào dé jīng　dì wǔ shí bā zhāng

其 政 闷 闷，其 民 淳 淳；其 政 察 察，其 民 缺 缺。
qí zhèng mēn mēn qí mín chún chún qí zhèng chá chá qí mín quē quē

祸 兮，福 之 所 倚；福 兮，祸 之 所 伏。
huò xī fú zhī suǒ yǐ fú xī huò zhī suǒ fú

孰 知 其 极? 其 无 正 也。正 复 为 奇，善 复 为 妖。
shú zhī qí jí qí wú zhèng yě zhèng fù wéi qí shàn fù wéi yāo

人 之 迷，其 日 固 久。
rén zhī mí qí rì gù jiǔ

是 以 圣 人 方 而 不 割，廉 而 不 刿，
shì yǐ shèng rén fāng ér bù gē lián ér bú guì

直 而 不 肆，光 而 不 耀。
zhí ér bú sì guāng ér bú yào

Fortune and misfortune are not absolute. So are normalcy and abnormalcy, and goodness and badness. Unaware of this, ordinary people can see only the positive without going a step further to explore the negative. That is why disasters come about when they pray for happiness.

Tao Te Ching
Chapter 59

In ruling the state and serving Heaven
Nothing is better than practising frugality.
Only through frugality
Can you identify with Tao.
This identification means constant virtuous cultivation.
With cultivated virtues nothing is impossible.
As nothing is impossible, you can never fathom its limits.
With such unlimited power,
The country is protected.
And only if protected in this Great Tao,
Can a country endure.
This is called Tao; the roots go deep and firm,
And thus live long.

《道德经》 第五十九章
dào dé jīng dì wǔ shí jiǔ zhāng

治人事天，莫若啬。
zhì rén shì tiān mò ruò sè

夫为啬，是谓早服；早服谓之重积德；
fū wéi sè shì wèi zǎo fú zǎo fú wèi zhī zhòng jī dé

重积德则无不克；无不克则莫知其极；
zhòng jī dé zé wú bú kè wú bú kè zé mò zhī qí jí

莫知其极，可以有国；有国之母，可以长久；
mò zhī qí jí kě yǐ yǒu guó yǒu guó zhī mǔ kě yǐ cháng jiǔ

是谓深根固柢，长生久视之道。
shì wèi shēn gēn gù dǐ chángshēng jiǔ shì zhī dào

Mental frugality means mental cultivation with the aim of sustaining and consolidating the foundation. To attain it, one should cultivate high virtues and thus come closer to Tao. This is the optimal principle for state administration.

Tao Te Ching
Chapter 60

Ruling a big country
Is like cooking small fish.
When the country is run by Tao,
Demons do not cause trouble.
Not that demons cause no trouble,
But that they are not harmful.
Not that they are not harmful,
But that the sage does not harm either.
Since they both do not harm,
All natural virtues return to the people.

《道 德 经》 第 六 十 章
dào dé jīng   dì liù shí zhāng

治 大 国，若 烹 小 鲜。
zhì dà guó   ruò pēng xiǎo xiān

以 道 莅 天 下，其 鬼 不 神；
yǐ dào lì tiān xià   qí guǐ bù shén

非 其 鬼 不 神，其 神 不 伤 人；
fēi qí guǐ bù shén   qí shén bù shāng rén

非 其 神 不 伤 人，圣 人 亦 不 伤 人。
fēi qí shén bù shāng rén shèng rén yì bù shāng rén

夫 两 不 相 伤，故 德 交 归 焉。
fū liǎng bù xiāng shāng gù dé jiāo guī yān

> Rulers should maintain consistency in policy measures because changing policies will surely cause trouble to the people.

Tao Te Ching
Chapter 61

Big countries are located downstream,
Where all rivers converge,
Like the mother of the world.
The female overcomes the male with serenity,
Taking serenity as modesty.
A big country draws a small one,
When it treats the latter cordially.
A small country wins the trust of a big one,
When it respects the latter.
Therefore, a modest big country wins a small one,
And a modest small country gets the favour of a big one.
The big country wants nothing but to gather more people,
While the small country wants to be protected.
Both the big and small countries can get what they want,
But the big one should be modest and tolerant.

《道 德 经》 第 六 十 一 章
dào dé jīng dì liù shí yī zhāng

大 邦 者 下 流，天 下 之 牝，天 下 之 交 也。
dà bāng zhě xià liú tiān xià zhī pìn tiān xià zhī jiāo yě

牝 常 以 静 胜 牡，以 静 为 下。
pìn cháng yǐ jìng shèng mǔ yǐ jìng wéi xià

故 大 邦 以 下 小 邦，则 取 小 邦；
gù dà bāng yǐ xià xiǎo bāng zé qǔ xiǎo bāng

小 邦 以 下 大 邦，则 取 大 邦。
xiǎo bāng yǐ xià dà bāng zé qǔ dà bāng

故 或 下 以 取，或 下 而 取。
gù huò xià yǐ qǔ huò xià ér qǔ

大 邦 不 过 欲 兼 畜 人，小 邦 不 过 欲 入 事 人。
dà bāng bú guò yù jiān chù rén xiǎo bāng bú guò yù rù shì rén

夫 两 者 各 得 所 欲，大 者 宜 为 下。
fū liáng zhě gè dé suǒ yù dà zhě yí wéi xià

Tao Te Ching
Chapter 62

Tao is the secret of everything.
A good man treasures it,
And a bad man seeks to keep it.
Good words can trade respect,
And good deeds can attract attention.
For a bad man,
How can he give up Tao?
Therefore, when the emperor ascends the throne,
Three princes are assigned,
And jewels presented and four-horse carriages paraded.
Yet nothing is better than showing him Tao.
Why did the ancients treasure Tao?
Isn't it because all needs can be met,
And all crimes can be forgiven?
Thus it is highly valued by the world.

《道德经》 第六十二章
dào dé jīng　　dì liù shí èr zhāng

道者万物之奥。善人之宝，不善人之所保。
dào zhě wàn wù zhī ào　　shàn rén zhī bǎo　bú shàn rén zhī suǒ bǎo

美言可以市尊，美行可以加人。
měi yán kě yi shì zūn　měi xíng kě yi jiā rén

人之不善，何弃之有? 故立天子，置三公，
rén zhī bú shàn hé qì zhī yǒu　gù lì tiān zi　zhì sān gōng

虽有拱璧以先驷马，不如坐进此道。
suī yǒu gǒng bì yi xiān sì mǎ　bù rú zuò jìn ci dào

古之所以贵此道者何?
gǔ zhī suǒ yi guì ci dào zhě hé

不曰:求以得，有罪以免邪? 故为天下贵。
bù yuē qiú yi dé　yǒu zuì yi miǎn yé　gù wéi tiān xià guì

All people are equal before Tao. Tao protects the good men, and does not cast aside the bad men. It can respond to all needs and help rectify all mistakes. This is where Tao counts.

Tao Te Ching
Chapter 63

Act without interference,
Do things non-artificially,
And taste the tasteless.
Big grows out of small and many out of few,
Return good for evil.
Deal with difficulties when they are easy,
Do great things when they are small.
All difficulties in the world,
Should be dealt with when easy;
All great things in the world,
Should be handled when small.
That is why the sage can accomplish great things,
Though he is always engaged in trivia.
Casual promises generate little trust,
Much ease leads to added difficulty.
That is why the sage, who considers everything difficult,
Ends up meeting no trouble.

《道德经》 第六十三章
dào dé jīng dì liù shí sān zhāng

为 无 为，事 无 事，味 无 味。
wéi wú wéi shì wú shì wèi wú wèi

大 小 多 少，报 怨 以 德。
dà xiǎo duō shǎo bào yuàn yǐ dé

图 难 于 其 易，为 大 于 其 细；
tú nán yú qí yì wéi dà yú qí xì

天 下 难 事，必 作 于 易，
tiān xià nán shì bì zuò yú yì

天 下 大 事，必 作 于 细。
tiān xià dà shì bì zuò yú xì

是 以 圣 人 终 不 为 大，故 能 成 其 大。
shì yǐ shèng rén zhōng bù wéi dà gù néng chéng qí dà

夫 轻 诺 必 寡 信，多 易 必 多 难。
fū qīng nuò bì guǎ xìn duō yì bì duō nán

是 以 圣 人 犹 难 之，故 终 无 难 矣。
shì yǐ shèng rén yóu nán zhī gù zhōng wú nán yǐ

To achieve something, you should take a flexible attitude, face life and take actions with a peaceful mind. You should also follow the order from small to big, scarce to plentiful, and easy to difficult.

Tao Te Ching
Chapter 64

What is stable is easy to retain,
What has not come about is easy to plan for,
What is fragile is easy to be broken,
What is small is easy to be scattered.
Do things when omens are still out of sight,
Manage affairs when they are in order.
A big tree grows
From a tiny sprout.
A nine-storey tower is built
From the first basket of earth.
A journey of a thousand miles
Begins with a single step.
Overdoing, you fail.
Possessive, you lose.
People usually frustrate their work
When success is around the corner.
Be careful from beginning to end,
You will not experience failure.
That is why the sage desires what others desire not,
And treasures not the rarities;
The sage studies what others do not study,
And corrects the mistakes made by the people
To aid the world as it is with no interference.

《道 德 经》 第 六 十 四 章
dào dé jīng dì liù shí sì zhāng

其 安 易 持，其 未 兆 易 谋。
qí ān yì chí qí wèi zhào yì móu

其 脆 易 泮，其 微 易 散。
qí cuì yì pàn qí wēi yì sàn

为 之 于 未 有，治 之 于 未 乱。
wéi zhī yú wèi yǒu zhì zhī yú wèi luàn

合 抱 之 木，生 于 毫 末；
hé bào zhī mù shēng yú háo mò

九 层 之 台，起 于 累 土；
jiǔ céng zhī tái qǐ yú lěi tǔ

千 里 之 行，始 于 足 下。
qiān li zhī xíng shǐ yú zú xià

为 者 败 之，执 者 失 之。
wéi zhě bài zhī zhí zhě shī zhī

民 之 从 事，常 于 几 成 而 败 之。
mín zhī cóng shì cháng yú jǐ chéng ér bài zhī

慎 终 如 始，则 无 败 事。
shèn zhōng rú shǐ zé wú bài shì

是 以 圣 人 欲 不 欲，不 贵 难 得 之 货；
shì yi shèng rén yù bú yù bú guì nán dé zhī huò

学 不 学，复 众 人 之 所 过，
xué bù xué fù zhòng rén zhī suǒ guò

以 辅 万 物 之 自 然 而 不 敢 为。
yi fǔ wàn wù zhī zì rán ér bù gǎn wéi

That which is big grows out of that which is small. Everything in the world follows a process of growth and development. Pay special attention to things that may escalate into some disasters.

Tao Te Ching
Chapter 65

The ancients who knew Tao well
Did not enlighten the people,
But rather kept them simple and guileless.
The people are difficult to rule
When they are clever.
If you rule the state with cleverness,
You are a usurper of state power.
If you do not rule that way,
The state will be blessed.
These two ideas are the norm in governing.
Constant awareness of the norm is called the "Subtle Virtue",
So deep and far-reaching is Virtue,
It returns everything to sincerity and simplicity,
And attains Great Harmony.

《道德经》 第六十五章
dào dé jīng　　dì liù shí wǔ zhāng

古 之 善 为 道 者，
gǔ　zhī　shàn wéi dào zhě

非 以 明 民，将 以 愚 之。
fēi　yǐ　míng mín　jiāng yǐ　yú　zhī

民 之 难 治，以 其 智 多。
mín zhī　nán zhì　yǐ　qí　zhì　duō

故 以 智 治 国，国 之 贼；
gù　yǐ　zhì　zhì guó　guó zhī zéi

不 以 智 治 国，国 之 福。
bù　yǐ　zhì　zhì guó　guó zhī fú

知 此 两 者 亦 稽 式。
zhī　cǐ　liáng zhě　yì　jī　shì

常 知 稽 式，是 谓"玄 德"。
cháng zhī jī　shì　shì wèi xuán dé

"玄 德" 深 矣，远 矣，与 物 反 矣，
xuán　dé　shēn yǐ　yuǎn yǐ　yǔ wù fǎn yǐ

然 后 乃 至 大 顺。
rán hòu　nǎi　zhì　dà shùn

People are difficult to manage because of the wiles they have acquired. Whether they are full of wiles or not depends on their rulers to a large degree.

When the rulers do not use wiles, the people will be guided to the path of simplicity and goodness. And only then will there be lasting peace in the world.

Tao Te Ching
Chapter 66

The river and sea are the lords of all valley streams,
Because they are located downstream.
That's why they can become their lords.
If the sage wants to rule over the people,
He should be humble in words to them.
If the sage wants to lead the people,
He should first put himself behind them.
That's why the sage placed above is not a burden to the people,
And the sage placed at the front is not an injury to them.
Therefore, the people are glad to support rather than despise him.
Because he does not contend,
Nobody in the world can contend with him.

《道德经》 第六十六章
dào dé jīng　　dì liù shí liù zhāng

江海之所以能为百谷王者，
jiāng hǎi zhī suǒ yǐ néng wéi bǎi gǔ wáng zhě

以其善下之，故能为百谷王。
yǐ qí shàn xià zhī　gù néng wéi bǎi gǔ wáng

是以圣人欲上民，必以言下之；
shì yǐ shèng rén yù shàng mín　bì yǐ yán xià zhī

欲先民，必以身后之。
yù xiān mín　bì yǐ shēn hòu zhī

是以圣人处上而民不重，处前而民不害。
shì yǐ shèng rén chǔ shàng ér mín bú zhòng chǔ qián ér mín bú hài

是以天下乐推而不厌。
shì yǐ tiān xià lè tuī ér bú yàn

以其不争，故天下莫能与之争。
yǐ qí bù zhēng gù tiān xià mò néng yǔ zhī zhēng

State administrators should keep a low profile first before they are positioned above. They should withdraw first before they become the pacesetter. Only when they are ready not to contend, can they become matchless. Similarly, only if they adhere to non-interference will they become capable of everything.

Tao Te Ching
Chapter 67

I am told by everybody:
Tao is great and unique.
Because it is great, it is unique.
If it is like anything,
It will become trivial soon.
I have three treasures,
Which I hold and cherish.
The first is compassion,
The second, frugality,
And the third, not daring to be ahead of others.
Being compassionate, I can be brave;
Being frugal, I can be rich;
Not daring to be ahead of others, I can achieve success.
I will die,
If I am brave without being compassionate,
Get rich without being frugal,
Or be adventurous without being cautious.
With compassion, I can win a battle
Or set up a strong defence.
When Heaven wants to save somebody,
It will protect him with compassion.

《道德经》 第六十七章
dào dé jīng dì liù shí qī zhāng

天下皆谓我："道大，似不肖。"夫唯大，故似不肖。
tiān xià jiē wèi wǒ   dào dà   sì bú xiào   fū wéi dà   gù sì bú xiào

若肖，久矣其细也夫！我有三宝，持而保之。
ruò xiào   jiǔ yǐ qí xì yě fū   wǒ yǒu sān bǎo   chí ér bǎo zhī

一曰慈，二曰俭，三曰不敢为天下先。
yī yuē cí   èr yuē jiǎn   sān yuē bù gǎn wéi tiān xià xiān

慈故能勇；俭故能广；不敢为天下先，故能成器长。
cí gù néng yǒng jiǎn gù néng guǎng bù gǎn wéi tiān xià xiān gù néng chéng qì zhǎng

今舍慈且勇；舍俭且广；舍后且先；死矣！
jīn shě cí qiě yǒng shě jiǎn qiě guǎng shě hòu qiě xiān   sǐ yǐ

夫慈以战则胜，以守则固。天将救之，以慈卫之。
fū cí yǐ zhàn zé shèng yǐ shǒu zé gù tiān jiāng jiù zhī yǐ cí wèi zhī

Among the three treasures, compassion is the most important. It can ensure a victory or a solid defence in war. When Heaven wants to help a man, it will instruct him to become compassionate.

Love and compassion are essential to the friendly coexistence of human beings. If everybody possesses the great love Heaven and Earth show towards the myriad things, all conflicts in the world will be resolved.

Tao Te Ching
Chapter 68

A good general is not belligerent,
A good fighter is not short-tempered,
A constant victor does not engage the enemy.
A good utiliser of talents places himself below.
This is called the virtue of non-contention,
The ability to make use of talents.
And also the means of following Tao.
This is the time-honoured supreme principle.

《道德经》 第六十八章
dào dé jīng dì liù shí bā zhāng

善为士者，不武；善战者，不怒；
shàn wéi shì zhě bù wǔ shàn zhàn zhě bú nù

善胜敌者，不与；善用人者，为之下。
shàn shèng dí zhě bù yǔ shàn yòng rén zhě wéi zhī xià

是谓不争之德，是谓用人之力，
shì wèi bù zhēng zhī dé shì wèi yòng rén zhī lì

是谓配天古之极。
shì wèi pèi tiān gǔ zhī jí

People should not flaunt their strength, fly into temper randomly and engage in direct conflict with others. They are expected to make full use of the talents and capabilities of others. By utilising the talents of others, one can attain the goal of contention through non-contention. This is a time-honoured principle that proves compatible with the way of Heaven.

Tao Te Ching
Chapter 69

A strategist once said:
"I would rather be provoked than to provoke,
I would rather retreat a foot than advance an inch."
This is called advancing without a formation,
Raising hands as if they are not seen,
Holding swords as if they are not visible,
And engaging the enemy as if they are nonexistent.
No danger is greater than being arrogant,
And arrogance can almost deprive a man of his treasures.
Thus, when two armies match each other in strength,
The one burning with righteous indignation will win.

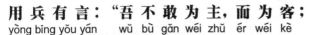

《道德经》 第六十九章
dào dé jīng　　dì liù shí jiǔ zhāng

用兵有言："吾不敢为主，而为客；
yòng bīng yǒu yán　　wú bù gǎn wéi zhǔ ér wéi kè

不敢进寸，而退尺。"
bù gǎn jìn cùn ér tuì chǐ

是谓行无行；攘无臂；扔无敌；执无兵。
shì wèi xíng wú xíng rǎng wú bì rēng wú dí zhí wú bīng

祸莫大于轻敌，轻敌几丧吾宝。
huò mò dà yú qīng dí qīng dí jǐ sàng wú bǎo

故抗兵相若，哀者胜矣。
gù kàng bīng xiāng ruò āi zhě shèng yǐ

A war is launched only when no other options can be found. When we have to face a war, we should refrain from indiscriminately provoking, attacking, underestimating or using weapons against the enemies.

Tao Te Ching
Chapter 70

My words are extremely easy to understand,
And extremely easy to put into practice.
Yet nobody comprehends them,
Or applies them into action.
My words have their source;
And my actions have their bases.
Because of their ignorance,
They cannot understand me.
Few people comprehend me,
And fewer people emulate me.
Thus the sage, dressed coarsely,
keeps a jewel in his bosom.

《道德经》 第七十章
dào dé jīng dì qī shí zhāng

吾 言 甚 易 知 , 甚 易 行 。
wú yán shèn yì zhī shèn yì xíng

天 下 莫 能 知 , 莫 能 行 。言 有 宗 ,事 有 君 。
tiān xià mò néng zhī mò néng xíng yán yǒu zōng shì yǒu jūn

夫 唯 无 知 , 是 以 不 我 知 。
fū wéi wú zhī shì yǐ bù wǒ zhī

知 我 者 希 , 则 我 者 贵 。是 以 圣 人 被 褐 而 怀 玉 。
zhī wō zhě xī zé wǒ zhě guì shì yǐ shèng rén pī hè ér huái yù

153

Tao Te Ching
Chapter 71

It's wise to know you do not know something.
It's foolish to pretend you know what you actually do not know.
When you recognise the foolishness of pretense,
You will be free of it.
The sage is not foolish.
He takes foolish acts seriously,
So he is not a fool.

《道德经》 第七十一章
dào dé jīng dì qī shí yī zhāng

知 不 知 , 尚 矣 ; 不 知 知 , 病 也 。
zhī bù zhī shàng yǐ bù zhī zhī bìng yě

圣 人 不 病 , 以 其 病 病 。
shēng rén bú bìng yǐ qí bìng bìng

夫 唯 病 病 , 是 以 不 病 。
fū wéi bìng bìng shì yǐ bú bìng

There are some people who have only a smattering of knowledge about something but pretend to know it inside out. With their attention fixed merely on the surface of things, they believe they have grasped the essence.

A true sage is one who not only knows himself but is able to examine himself honestly as well.

Tao Te Ching
Chapter 72

When people no longer fear your might,
A disaster is on the way.
Do not disturb the people's homes,
Do not make it hard for them to live.
Because of no pressure,
There is no resentment.
Thus, the sage knows himself,
Yet does not show off.
The sage cherishes himself
Yet does not overprize himself.
Thus he abandons that for this.

《道 德 经》 第 七 十 二 章

dào dé jīng dì qī shí èr zhāng

民 不 畏 威，则 大 威 至。

mín bú wèi wēi zé dà wēi zhì

无 狎 其 所 居，无 厌 其 所 生。

wú xiá qí suǒ jū wú yàn qí suǒ shēng

夫 唯 不 厌，是 以 不 厌。

fū wéi bú yàn shì yǐ bú yàn

是 以 圣 人 自 知 不 自 见；自 爱 不 自 贵。

shì yǐ shèng rén zì zhī bú zì xiàn zì ài bú zì guì

故 去 彼 取 此。

gù qù bǐ qǔ cǐ

Rulers should have a clear self-knowledge and should not adopt a high-handed policy of oppressing and exploiting the people without scruple. When the people entertain no fear of their cruel domination, they will rise up in an awe-inspiring resistance.

Tao Te Ching
Chapter 73

If you are brave and daring you will die.
If you are brave yet remain calm you will survive.
These two types of being brave,
One is beneficial and the other is harmful,
Who knows
Why Heaven loathes something?
The question is even beyond the sage.
Tao of Heaven is to win without striving,
To respond without words,
To have things come naturally without summoning,
To plan without getting anxious.
The net of Heaven is big and vast,
It is loose yet nothing can slip through.

《道德经》 第七十三章
dào dé jīng   dì qī shí sān zhāng

勇于敢则杀，勇于不敢则活。
yǒng yú gǎn zé shā yǒng yú bù gǎn zé huó

此两者，或利或害。
cǐ liǎng zhě huò lì huò hài

天之所恶，孰知其故？
tiān zhī suǒ wù shú zhī qí gù

天之道，不争而善胜，
tiān zhī dào bù zhēng ér shàn shèng

不言而善应，不召而自来，繟然而善谋。
bù yán ér shàn yìng bù zhāo ér zì lái chǎn rán ér shàn móu

天网恢恢，疏而不失。
tiān wǎng huī huī shū ér bú shī

Under the Law of Nature, weakness and non-interference are promoted. Human behaviour should be governed by the law of Nature and all reckless and combative acts should be prohibited.

Tao Te Ching
Chapter 74

If the people are not afraid of death
How can they be threatened by it?
To make the people fear death,
A man should be sentenced to death
If he commits a crime.
Then who dares to become a criminal?
Usually, the death sentence is carried out by an executioner.
If you take the executioner's place,
It's like cutting wood for the carpenter.
When you cut wood for the carpenter,
Chances are you will injure your hands.

《道德经》 第七十四章
dào dé jīng dì qī shí sì zhāng

民 不 畏 死，奈 何 以 死 惧 之？
mín bú wèi sǐ nài hé yǐ sǐ jù zhī

若 使 民 常 畏 死，而 为 奇 者，吾 得 执 而 杀 之，孰 敢？
ruò shǐ mín cháng wèi sǐ ér wéi qí zhě wú dé zhí ér shā zhī shú gǎn

常 有 司 杀 者 杀。夫 代 司 杀 者 杀，是 谓 代 大 匠 斫，
cháng yǒu sī shā zhě shā fū dài sī shā zhě shā shì wèi dài dà jiàng zhuó

夫 代 大 匠 斫 者，希 有 不 伤 其 手 矣。
fū dài dà jiàng zhuó zhě xī yǒu bù shāng qí shǒu yǐ

Life and death in the natural world are meted out according to their own law. Rulers are not needed to kill people for Heaven by brutal means. He who kills in the capacity of Heaven will end up injured himself.

161

Tao Te Ching
Chapter 75

The people starve,
Because the rulers overtax them.
So they starve.
The people are difficult to govern,
Because the rulers act irrationally.
So they are difficult to govern.
The people do not take death seriously,
Because the rulers cherish their own lives too much.
So they do not take death seriously.
He who does not strive for his own life
Is wiser than he who values highly his own life.

《道德经》 第七十五章
dào dé jīng　　 dì qī shí wǔ zhāng

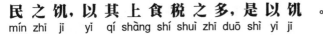

民 之 饥，以 其 上 食 税 之 多，是 以 饥 。
mín zhī jī　yi　qí shàng shí shuì zhī duō shì yi jī

民 之 难 治，以 其 上 之 有 为，是 以 难 治。
mín zhī nán zhì　yi　qí shàng zhī yǒu wéi　shì yi nán zhì

民 之 轻 死，以 其 上 求 生 之 厚，是 以 轻 死。
mín zhī qīng si　yi　qí shàng qiú shēng zhī hòu　shì yi qīng si

夫 唯 无 以 生 为 者，是 贤 于 贵 生。
fū　wéi wú yi shēng wéi zhě shì xián yú guì shēng

Tao Te Ching
Chapter 76

In life people are gentle and weak,
At death they become hard and stiff.
Growing plants are soft and delicate,
They become withered and dried up at death.
Therefore, the hard and stiff dies,
While the soft and weak survives.
An army, if strong, is wiped out,
And a tree, if thick, is cut down.
The strong is inferior,
While the weak is superior.

《道德经》 第七十六章
dào dé jīng　　dì qī shí liù zhāng

人之生也柔弱，其死也坚强。
rén zhī shēng yě róu ruò　qí sǐ yě jiān qiáng

草木之生也柔脆，其死也枯槁。
cǎo mù zhī shēng yě róu cuì　qí sǐ yě kū gǎo

故坚强者死之徒，柔弱者生之徒。
gù jiān qiáng zhě sǐ zhī tú　róu ruò zhě shēng zhī tú

是以兵强则灭，木强则折。
shì yǐ bīng qiáng zé miè　mù qiáng zé zhé

强大处下，柔弱处上。
qiáng dà chǔ xià　róu ruò chǔ shàng

165

Tao Te Ching
Chapter 77

Does Tao of Heaven work like pulling a bow?
The bow, when depressed, the top is lowered, the bottom is raised.
A long string is cut short,
A short string is extended.
Tao of Heaven
Is to reduce the excess and supplement the shortage.
The way of man is different,
It is to reduce what is short and increase the excess.
Who can offer his excess to the world?
None other than a follower of Tao.
Therefore the sage acts without becoming dependent,
Accomplishes without becoming conceited,
And refrains from showing his virtues and talent.

《道 德 经》 第 七 十 七 章
dào dé jīng   dì qī shí qī zhāng

天 之 道, 其 犹 张 弓 与?
tiān zhī dào qí yóu zhāng gōng yú

高 者 抑 之, 下 者 举 之;
gāo zhī yì zhī xià zhě jǔ zhī

有 余 者 损 之, 不 足 者 补 之。
yǒu yú zhě sǔn zhī bù zú zhě bǔ zhī

天 之 道, 损 有 余 而 补 不 足。
tiān zhī dào sǔn yǒu yú ér bǔ bù zú

人 之 道, 则 不 然, 损 不 足 以 奉 有 余。
rén zhī dào zé bù rán sǔn bù zú yǐ fèng yǒu yú

孰 能 有 余 以 奉 天 下, 唯 有 道 者。
shú néng yǒu yú yǐ fèng tiān xià wéi yǒu dào zhě

是 以 圣 人 为 而 不 恃, 功 成 而 不 处, 其 不 欲 见 贤。
shì yǐ shèng rén wéi ér bù shì gōng chéng ér bú chù qí bú yù jiàn xián

The natural law is in favour of supplementing what is lacking with what is in surplus so that equilibrium and harmony are maintained. This should be followed in formulating rules and regulations for a perfect and harmonious society.

Tao Te Ching
Chapter 78

Nothing in the world
Is softer and weaker than water,
Yet nothing outdoes it in overcoming the hard and strong.
This is because nothing can replace it.
It is a fact
That the weak can overcome the strong,
And the soft can defeat the hard,
Yet nobody can achieve it.
Thus the sage remarks:
"He who can accept national humiliation,
Is called the ruler of a state.
He who can bear national disasters,
Is called the governor of the world."
Truth sounds conflicting.

《道德经》 第七十八章
dào dé jīng　　 dì qī shí bā zhāng

天下莫柔弱于水，
tiān xià mò róu ruò yú shuǐ

而攻坚强者莫之能胜，以其无以易之。
ér gōng jiān qiáng zhě mò zhī néng shèng yǐ qí wú yǐ yì zhī

弱之胜强，柔之胜刚，
ruò zhī shèng qiáng róu zhī shèng gāng

天下莫不知，莫能行。
tiān xià mò bù zhī　 mò néng xíng

是以圣人云："受国之垢，是谓社稷主；
shì yǐ shèng rén yún　　 shòu guó zhī gòu　 shì wèi shè jì zhǔ

受国不祥，是为天下王。"
shòu guó bù xiáng shì wèi tiān xià wáng

正言若反。
zhèng yán ruò fǎn

Therefore, a true ruler is able to take responsibility for national humiliation and face up to national disasters. Rulers should cultivate water-like qualities before they can win the state and the world as well.

Tao Te Ching
Chapter 79

A big dispute can be pacified,
But resentments always remain.
How can this be deemed a kind gesture?
Thus, the sage keeps the deed of loan,
Yet never demands repayment.
A man of virtue keeps the deed,
And a crooked man acts like a tax collector.
Tao of Heaven is impartial,
And it often helps the good people.

《道德经》 第七十九章
dào dé jīng dì qī shí jiǔ zhāng

和大怨,必有余怨;安可以为善?
hé dà yuàn bì yǒu yú yuàn ān kě yi wéi shàn

是以圣人执左契,而不责于人。
shì yi shèng rén zhí zuǒ qì ér bù zé yú rén

有德司契,无德司彻。
yǒu dé sī qì wú dé sī chè

天道无亲,常与善人。
tiān dào wú qīn cháng yǔ shàn rén

Rulers should not incur resentments from the people by exploiting them with taxes and controlling them with stringent laws. An ideal administration practises "effortless" governance, educates the people with virtue, gives without taking and does not interfere in the people's affairs.

171

Tao Te Ching
Chapter 80

Let there be a small country with a small population.
Implements are not used while thousands of them are available.
People cherish their lives and do not want to travel afar.
Having boats and carriages, they do not ride in them.
With armours and weapons, they do not use them.
People resume taking notes with knots.
Let them have sweet food,
Wear nice clothes,
Enjoy their family life,
And delight in customs.
Neighbouring countries can be seen,
And dogs and chickens can be heard,
Yet they would not visit each other throughout their lives.

《道 德 经》 第 八 十 章
dào dé jīng   dì bā shí zhāng

小 国 寡 民。
xiǎo guó guǎ mín

使 有 什 伯 之 器 而 不 用；
shǐ yǒu shén bó zhī qì ér bú yòng

使 民 重 死 而 不 远 徙。
shǐ mín zhòng sǐ ér bù yuǎn xi

虽 有 舟 舆，无 所 乘 之，虽 有 甲 兵，无 所 陈 之。
suī yǒu zhōu yú   wú suǒ chéng zhī   suī yǒu jiǎ bīng   wú suǒ chén zhǐ

使 民 复 结 绳 而 用 之。
shǐ mín fù   jié shéng ér yòng zhī

甘 其 食，美 其 服，安 其 居，乐 其 俗。
gān qí shí měi qí fú ān qí jū   lè qí sú

邻 国 相 望，鸡 犬 之 声 相 闻，
lín   guó xiāng wàng jī   quǎn zhī shēng xiāng wén

民 至 老 死，不 相 往 来。
mín zhì lǎo sǐ   bù xiāng wǎng lái

People can get along well with one another because of their pure good nature. Here, the people are simple and guileless and they do not have to rush about or take risks to make a living. Military war, which is based on the jungle law, does not break out here. Therefore, life is stable and simple.

Tao Te Ching
Chapter 81

True words are strident,
Sweet words are insincere.
A good man does not debate.
A debater is not a good man.
A learned man is not well-read,
A well-read man is not learned.
The sage does not accumulate,
The more he helps others,
the more meaningful his life is.
The more he gives, the more he gets,
Tao of Heaven
Is to benefit and not to harm.
Tao of the Sage,
Is to act and not to strive.

《道德经》 第八十一章
dào dé jīng dì bā shí yī zhāng

信言不美，美言不信。
xìn yán bù měi měi yán bú xìn

善者不辩，辩者不善。
shàn zhě bú biàn biàn zhě bú shàn

知者不博，博者不知。
zhī zhě bù bó bó zhě bù zhī

圣人不积，既以为人己愈有，既以与人己愈多。
shèng rén bù jī jǐ yǐ wèi rén jǐ yù yǒu jǐ yǐ yǔ rén jǐ yù duō

天之道，利而不害；圣人之道，为而不争。
tiān zhī dào lì ér bú hài shèng rén zhī dào wéi ér bù zhēng

Heaven operates in a way that is beneficial rather than harmful to everything in the world. The sage adheres to the principle of bringing benefit to the people instead of vying with them. The loftiest realm of life lies in the combination of truth, goodness and beauty, with truth at the core. The sage acts based on Tao, helping and giving without struggling for personal fame and gain. This is exactly the crowning code of human conduct and also an act of great virtue.

The
Essence
of Tao

wú wéi 无为

Wu-wei: a key term in *Tao Te Ching*, appearing more than 10 times (See Appendix 2).

Chapter 2	The sage acts effortlessly, And teaches not by words. The myriad things rise and fall unobstructed. The world is created but not possessed, Deeds are performed yet not for ostentation. This is accomplishing without pretension. Because of such non-pretension, The accomplishments will never be removed.
Chapter 3	If you act without striving, nothing is beyond manageability.
Chapter 10	Ruling the state with a kind heart, can you achieve non-interference?
Chapter 29	The sage does not overdo, so he does not fail, and the sage is not possessive, so he does not lose.
Chapter 37	The eternal Tao does not exert itself yet it is capable of doing everything.
Chapter 38	Higher virtue is non-interfering and non-motivated, lower virtue is interfering and motivated.
Chapter 43	The softest thing in the world is able to run in and out of the hardest thing. The invisible can penetrate the densest, thus I know the benefit of inaction.
Chapter 48	In studying, progress is made every day. In practising Tao, loss is incurred every day. Loss upon loss, till non-action is attained, nothing is done yet everything is accomplished. To rule the world non-intervention should be used, when intervention takes place, the world cannot be ruled well.
Chapter 57	The sages say: "I am not coercive, and the people become civilised themselves. I delight in silence, and the people improve. Act without interference, do things non-artificially, and taste the tasteless. themselves.
Chapter 63	Act without interference, do things non-artificially, and taste the tasteless.

1. As a verb, it means "to not act rashly", conforming to the natural course of development, and doing what should be done instead of overdoing for artificial purposes.

2. As a noun, it refers to basic and natural acts.

3. *Wu-wei* embodies a political and administrative concept which Lao Zi promoted energetically. As a witness to reckless governments which had brought disasters on the people, he appealed to rulers in the hope that they would adopt a policy of non-interference which grants peace and freedom to the people.

zì rán 自然

Another key term in *Tao Te Ching* which appears at five places (See Appendix 3).

Chapter 17	When things are accomplished, the people say in unison: we have acted naturally.
Chapter 23	To speak less is natural.
Chapter 25	Man emulates Earth, Earth emulates Heaven, Heaven emulates Tao and Tao emulates nature.
Chapter 51	That Tao is respectable, and Virtue is valuable, is spontaneous rather than forced.
Chapter 64	That is why the sage desires what others desire not, and treasures not the rarities; the sage studies what others do not study, and corrects the mistakes made by the people to aid the world as it is with no interference.

1. As a noun, it has two meanings. First, it means the natural or real aspect of a person, place, or thing. This is the primary meaning. Second, it means the material world and its phenomena.

2. As a verb, it means "to come into being in a natural or spontaneous way" as in "The people say in unison: We have acted naturally." (Chapter 17)

3. Lao Zi advocates "Tao emulates Nature." From the ontological perspective, Lao Zi believes that this world exists and operates according to its own laws and thus independent of human will. Considered from the theory of practice, he maintains that men cannot succeed unless they respect and observe the natural laws.

xū jìng 虚静

Lao Zi said, "Attain the ultimate emptiness / Hold fast to a mind of peace." (Chapter 16), which means that the origin of all things exists in a state of emptiness and serenity. We should deal with all things in a state of emptiness and serenity.

1. As the root all things, emptiness means "infinity". Serenity refers to the state of emptiness — being silent, having no desire and remaining tranquil.

2. In Lao Zi's opinion, emptiness and serenity constitute the foundation of life and politics. In life, one needs to "attain the ultimate emptiness, / hold fast to a mind of peace". In state administration, "peace and quietude come before everything". By keeping "insatiable desire" at bay, we will be able to liberate our lives from labour and suffering, and state rulers will be able to govern the state and the people well.

róu ruò 柔弱

Lao Zi employs many metaphors in *Tao Te Ching* to put across his concept of "soft and weak" (See Appendix 4).

Chapter 36	The weak can outdo the strong.
Chapter 76	In life people are gentle and weak, at death they become hard and stiff. Growing plants are soft and delicate, they become withered and dried up at death. Therefore, the hard and stiff dies, while the soft and weak survives. An army, if strong, is wiped out, and a tree, if thick, is cut down. The strong is inferior, while the weak is superior.
Chapter 78	Nothing in the world is softer and weaker than water, yet nothing outdoes it in overcoming the hard and strong. This is because nothing can replace it. The weak can overcome the strong, and the soft can defeat the hard, yet nobody can achieve it.

1. Soft and weak: Human body — which is soft when alive and becomes stiff and hard after decease. Our teeth are hard yet will fall off. Our tongues are soft yet able to live long.

Grass and trees — tall trees will be cut down, or break and even be uprooted when a typhoon comes. In contrast, grass is soft and delicate yet will not break, and can dance with the wind.

2. For Lao Zi, all human strifes and conflicts arise from men's competitiveness, conceit and self-importance. Thus, men should have a "soft and weak", "modest" and "non-competitive" mind before they can resolve all conflicts and disputes and build a harmonious society.

Lao Zi is also of the opinion that soft and weak stand in confrontation with hard and strong; soft can overcome hard and weak can prevail over strong; and water constantly dripping can wear holes in stone.

What Lao Zi promotes is a philosophy of life. Here, soft is a major property of life and all affirmations of, and praises for, soft also apply to life.

The softest thing in the world is able to penetrate the sturdiest thing.

bù zhēng 不争

Bu-zheng appears seven times in *Tao Te Ching* (See Appendix 5).

Chapter 3	If the worthy is not exalted, you will not create competition among people.
Chapter 8	Ultimate kindness is like water. Water benefits rather than rivals with everything. Such a person resides in a place hideous to all. He is thus close to Tao. He inhabits the lowland; his mind is as calm as the abyss, he associates with others kindly, he honours his words, he governs well, he handles affairs properly, he never lets go of good opportunities, since he does not compete, he is free of errors.
Chapter 22	Because he does not contend, none can contend with him.
Chapter 66	Because he does not contend, nobody in the world can contend with him.
Chapter 68	A good general is not belligerent, a good fighter is not short-tempered, a constant victor does not engage the enemy. A good utiliser of talents places himself below. This is called the virtue of non-contention, the ability to make use of talents. And also the means of following Tao. This is the time-honoured supreme principle.
Chapter 73	Tao of Heaven is to win without striving, to respond without words, to have things come naturally without summoning, to plan without getting anxious. The net of Heaven is big and vast, It is loose yet nothing can slip through.
Chapter 81	Tao of Heaven is to benefit and not to harm. Tao of the Sage, is to act and not to strive.

1. Bu-zheng: means "not to strive". Lao Zi hopes that people can make their efforts in a natural way in an unequal society without possessing themselves of the results thus achieved. This represents a great moral spirit that benefits everything in the world and serves others' interests without fighting for fame and gain with them.

2. On the basis of this, Lao Zi proposes the concept of "low positioning" which is built on the concept of "soft and weak" and "non-competitive". Being aware of people's tendency to stand at high and bright positions, he promotes the idea of placing oneself in a low place, and not controlling and possessing people and things. In so doing, all conflicts and disputes will be resolved readily. Moreover, this attitude can also help people develop the quality of tolerance and other moral qualities.

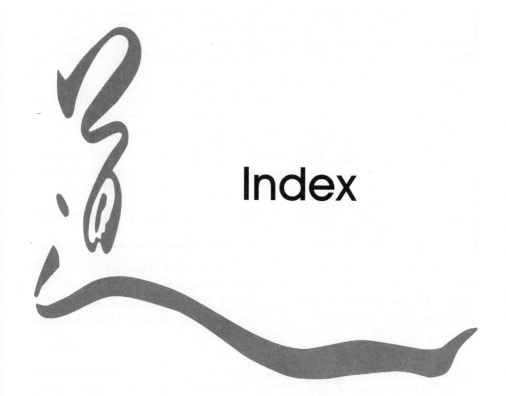

Index

Appendix 1: Notes on *Tao*

Order*	Chapter	pg no.	English translation of *Tao Te Ching*
1 - 3	1	14	Tao, if articulable, is not the eternal Tao.
4	4	20	Tao is void and shapeless, yet its power unlimited. So profound; it is the origin of the myriad things!
5	8	28	Water benefits rather than rivals with everything. Such a person resides in a place hideous to all. He is thus close to Tao.
6	9	30	Having more than enough, is worse than having nothing. A knife sharpened too much, does not last long. A house full of gold and jadestones, cannot be guarded for long. A pretentious man of means, incurs misfortunes. Retire upon achieving success, this is the way of heaven.
7-8	14	40	Catch hold of the ancient Tao to manage what is available now, to know the origin of everything. This is called the essence of Tao.
9	15	42	The ancients who knew Tao were of mysterious perception and inexpressible profundity. Because they were unfathomable, they were portrayed in a fashion: they were cautious like one crossing the river in winter, vigilant like one afraid of his neighbours, respectful like a guest, slack like ice about to thaw, simple like a piece of unprocessed wood, Broad-minded like a valley, and dim-witted like muddy water. Muddy water, when staying still awhile, will become clear soon. Still, when starting to move, will change step by step. The follower of Tao does not seek fullness. Because of this lack of fullness, he can retain the old. And get the new at once.
10 -11	16	44	Attain the ultimate emptiness, hold fast to a mind of peace. Knowing brings tolerance, tolerance makes justice, justice results in kingly miens, kingly miens conforms to heavenly principle, heavenly principle complies with Tao. Tao endures, no danger comes in your life.
12	18	48	When the great Tao is discarded, humanity and justice appear. When intellect is acquired, serious hypocrisy and deception come along.
13 -14	21	54	Acts of great virtue conform entirely to Tao. The thing called "Tao" is misty and hazy.
15 -17	23	58	To speak less is natural. A gale does not blow a whole morning, a shower does not last a whole day. What makes them so? Heaven and Earth. If Heaven and Earth cannot have them last long, let alone men. Therefore, people who follow Tao, are united with Tao; those who are united with Tao, are readily accepted by Tao.

* Order of appearance of *Tao* in the original Chinese *Tao Te Ching*.

Order*	Chapter	pg no.	English translation of *Tao Te Ching*
18 -19	24	60	Standing on tiptoe, you cannot keep balance. Striding forward, you cannot go far. if you are ostentatious you will not be self-conscious; if you are self-important you will not become well known; If you are boastful you will not become accomplished; if you are self-conceited you will not shine. Measured against Tao, these acts are leftovers and warts, disgusting to people, and a man who knows Tao will not commit such acts.
20 -23	25	62	Something is made from mixing things. It was born before Heaven and Earth. Not knowing its name, I describe it as "Tao", and name it "the Great" in a fashion. Thus, Tao is great, Heaven is great, Earth is great, and man is great. There are four great things in the universe, and man is one of them. Man emulates Earth, Earth emulates Heaven, Heaven emulates Tao. And Tao emulates Nature.
24 -26	30	72	If you assist the king with Tao, you will not resort to force of arms. Military action would fire back in the end. Where the army has camped, thorns and brambles grow wild. At the heels of a war comes a year of famine. Therefore, a good commander seeks only the end, and never flaunts his military strength. Victorious, he does not puff up, or become conceited, or become arrogant. He deems the victory inevitable, and never flaunts his superiority. Things start to age when they are strong, this is called a violation of Tao. Premature death befalls things that go against Tao.
27	31	74	Weapons are ominous, and nobody likes them. Therefore they have no use for a man of Tao. Weapons are inauspicious, and not intended for a gentleman. Even when he has to use them, he does not take them seriously. Victory thus won is not to be applauded, if applauded, the victor enjoys killing.
28	32	76	Tao is eternal, though it is nameless and unvarnished. Insignificant as it looks, nothing in the world can subjugate it. When Heaven and Earth are married, sweet dew will fall. Under no external order, it is dispersed evenly on earth. Things are created and names given, with names given, Heaven knows when to stop, and keep away from perils. The relationship of Tao and the world is like that of valley streams and rivers and seas.
29	34	80	Tao is a vast river, it can run both left and right. The myriad things live on it without being declined. It accomplishes a lot but never seeks fame and ownership.
30	35	82	Grasping the Great Image, the world will surrender itself. With the world surrendered yet unharmed, peace and stability will ensue. For music and delicacies, passersby stop. Tao, when uttered, tastes bland and dull.

* Order of appearance of *Tao* in the original Chinese *Tao Te Ching*.

Order*	Chapter	pg no.	English translation of *Tao Te Ching*
31	37	86	The eternal Tao does not exert itself Yet it is capable of doing everything.
32 -33	38	88	Higher virtue is non-interfering and non-motivated, lower virtue is interfering and motivated. Therefore, Tao is lost and Virtue brought in, the so-called "prescient" are merely flowers of Tao, heralding foolishness.
34 -35	40	92	Reversion is the movement of Tao, and being soft is its function.
36 -44	41	94	When superior men hear of Tao, they work hard to practise it. When average men hear of Tao, they regard it with suspicion. When inferior men hear of Tao, they deride it. Tao cannot be so called unless derided, therefore an aphorism has it: the bright path looks dark, advancing seems retreating, and the flat path looks bumpy. Tao is grand but nameless. So, only Tao, begins well and ends perfect.
45	42	96	Tao creates one, one creates two. Two creates three, and three creates everything in the world.
46 -47	46	104	When Tao prevails in a country, steeds are used to pull dung-carts. When Tao is discarded, ponies are born at the border.
48	47	106	Identify the way of Heaven without looking through the window.
49	48	108	In studying, progress is made every day. In practising Tao, loss is incurred every day. Loss upon loss, till non-action is attained,
50 -53	51	114	Tao gives birth to everything, Virtue raises it, the matter shapes it, and utilities materialise it. Hence, Tao is widely respected and Virtue highly valued. That Tao is respectable, and Virtue is valuable, is spontaneous rather than forced. Thus, Tao gives birth to everything, Virtue raises it, promoting its growth. Stimulating its maturity, nourishing and protecting it,
54 -56	53	118	If I possess a bit of knowledge, I will walk along the Great Tao, lest I stray from it. The Great Tao is flat, whereas people tend to take a winding path. When the court is corrupt, the farmland goes fallow and the granaries become empty. Dressed elegantly, wearing sharp swords, satiated with drink and food, and having extra wealth, This is what a ringleader is like. And certainly this goes against Tao!
57 -58	55	122	Vitality driven by desire is called presumptuousness. Things start to age when they are strong, this is called violation of Tao. Premature death befalls things contrary to Tao.
59	59	130	This is called Tao; the roots go deep and firm, and thus live long.

* Order of appearance of *Tao* in the original Chinese *Tao Te Ching*.

Order*	Chapter	pg no.	English translation of *Tao Te Ching*
60	60	132	Ruling a big country Is like cooking small fish. When the country is run by Tao, demons do not cause trouble.
61 -63	62	136	Tao is the secret of everything. Therefore, when the emperor ascends the throne, three princes are assigned, and jewels presented and four-horse carriages paraded. Yet nothing is better than showing him Tao. Why did the ancients treasure Tao? Isn't it because all needs can be met, and all crimes can be forgiven? Thus it is highly valued by the world.
64	65	142	The ancients who knew Tao well did not enlighten the people, but rather kept them simple and guileless.
65	67	146	I am told by everybody: Tao is great and unique. Because it is great, it is unique. If it is like anything, it will become trivial soon. I have three treasures, which I hold and cherish. The first is compassion, the second, frugality, and the third, not daring to be ahead of others. Being compassionate, I can be brave; being frugal, I can be rich; not daring to be ahead of others, I can achieve success. I will die, if I am brave without being compassionate, get rich without being frugal, or be adventurous without being cautious. With compassion, I can win a battle or set up a strong defence. When Heaven wants to save somebody, it will protect him with compassion.
66	73	158	Tao of Heaven is to win without striving, to respond without words.
67 -70	77	166	Does Tao of Heaven work like pulling a bow? The bow, when depressed, the top is lowered, the bottom is raised. A long string is cut short, a short string is extended. Tao of Heaven is to reduce the excess and supplement the shortage. The way of man is different, it is to reduce what is short and increase the excess. Who can offer his excess to the world? None other than a follower of Tao.
71	79	170	Tao of Heaven is impartial, and it often helps the good people.
72 -73	81	174	Tao of Heaven is to benefit and not to harm. Tao of the Sage, is to act and not to strive.

* Order of appearance of *Tao* in the original Chinese *Tao Te Ching*.

Appendix 2: Notes on *Wu-wei*

Order*	Chapter	pg no.	English translation of *Tao Te Ching*
1	2	16	Thus the sage acts effortlessly, and teaches not by words. The myriad things rise and fall unobstructed. The world is created but not possessed, deeds are performed yet not for ostentation. This is accomplishing without pretension. Because of such non-pretension, the accomplishments will never be removed.
2	3	18	If you act without striving, nothing is beyond manageability.
3	10	32	Ruling the state with a kind heart, can you achieve non-interference?
4	29	70	Thus the sage does not overdo, so he does not fail, and the sage is not possessive, so he does not lose.
5	37	86	The eternal Tao does not exert itself yet it is capable of doing everything.
6 -7	38	88	Higher virtue is non-interfering and non-motivated, lower virtue is interfering and motivated.
8	43	98	The softest thing in the world Is able to run in and out of the hardest thing. The invisible can penetrate the densest, thus I know the benefit of inaction. Teaching without words, gain without action, can hardly be achieved by anything in the world.
9 -10	48	108	In studying, progress is made every day. In practising Tao, loss is incurred every day. Loss upon loss, till non-action is attained, nothing is done yet everything is accomplished. To rule the world non-intervention should be used, when intervention takes place, the world cannot be ruled well.
11	57	126	Thus the sages say: "I am not coercive, and the people become civilised themselves. I delight in silence, and the people improve themselves. I do not interfere, and the people get rich themselves. I am not greedy, and the people become natural and guileless."
12	63	138	Act without interference, do things non-artificially, and taste the tasteless.

* Order of appearance of *Wu-wei* in the original Chinese *Tao Te Ching*.

Appendix 3: Notes on *Zi-ran*

Order*	Chapter	pg no.	English translation of *Tao Te Ching*
1	17	46	When things are accomplished, the people say in unison: we have acted naturally.
2	23	58	To speak less is natural.
3	25	62	Man emulates Earth, Earth emulates Heaven, Heaven emulates Tao and Tao emulates aature.
4	51	114	That Tao is respectable, and Virtue is valuable, is spontaneous rather than forced.
5	64	140	That is why the sage desires what others desire not, and treasures not the rarities; the sage studies what others do not study, and corrects the mistakes made by the people to aid the world as it is with no interference.

* Order of appearance of *Zi-ran* in the original Chinese *Tao Te Ching*.

Appendix 4: Notes on *Rou-ruo*

Order*	Chapter	pg no.	English translation of *Tao Te Ching*
1	36	84	The weak can outdo the strong.
2 - 4	76	164	In life people are gentle and weak, at death they become hard and stiff. Growing plants are soft and delicate, they become withered and dried up at death. Therefore, the hard and stiff dies, while the soft and weak survives. An army, if strong, is wiped out, and a tree, if thick, is cut down. The strong is inferior, while the weak is superior.
5	78	168	Nothing in the world is softer and weaker than water, yet nothing outdoes it in overcoming the hard and strong. This is because nothing can replace it. The weak can overcome the strong, and the soft can defeat the hard, yet nobody can achieve it.

* Order of appearance of *Rou-ruo* in the original Chinese *Tao Te Ching*.

Appendix 5: Notes on *Bu-zheng*

Order*	Chapter	pg no.	English translation of *Tao Te Ching*
1	3	18	If the worthy is not exalted, you will not create competition among people.
2	8	28	Ultimate kindness is like water. Water benefits rather than rivals with everything. Such a person resides in a place hideous to all. He is thus close to Tao. He inhabits the lowland; his mind is as calm as the abyss, he associates with others kindly, he honours his words, he governs well, he handles affairs properly, he never lets go of good opportunities, since he does not compete, he is free of errors.
3	22	56	Because he does not contend, none can contend with him.
4	66	144	Because he does not contend, nobody in the world can contend with him.
5	68	148	A good general is not belligerent, a good fighter is not short-tempered, a constant victor does not engage the enemy. A good utiliser of talents places himself below. This is called the virtue of non-contention, the ability to make use of talents. And also the means of following Tao. This is the time-honoured supreme principle.
6	73	158	Tao of Heaven is to win without striving, to respond without words, to have things come naturally without summoning, to plan without getting anxious. The net of Heaven is big and vast, it is loose yet nothing can slip through.
7	81	174	Tao of Heaven is to benefit and not to harm. Tao of the Sage, is to act and not to strive.

* Order of appearance of *Bu-zheng* in the original Chinese *Tao Te Ching*.

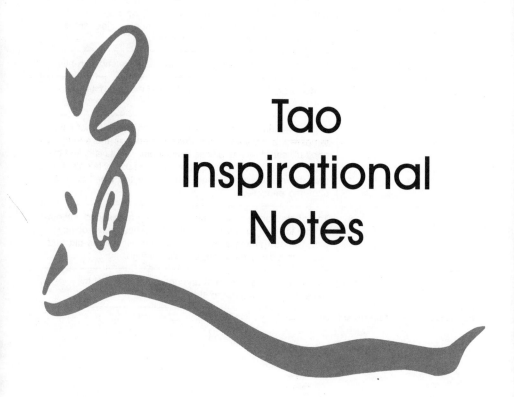

Tao
Inspirational
Notes

Non-Interfering

The eternal Tao does not not exert itself
Yet it is capable of doing everything.
— Tao Te Ching (Chapter 37)

You're abandoning good for evil because of a strong personal desire. You'll destroy yourself this way.

The state-administering concept of "non-interference" has been adopted by entrepreneurs in corporate management. Is it possible, then, to apply the concept also as a career guide directing us towards success?

The hard and stiff have lost their vitality, whereas the soft and weak remain strong and energetic

The weak can outdo the strong.
— Tao Te Ching (Chapter 36)
Therefore, the hard and stiff dies
while the soft and weak survives.
— Tao Te Ching (Chapter 76)

Disputes arise often in our daily life. Do you act like a domineering lord or treat people around you cordially and kindly? Are you modest and open-minded, or aggressive and belligerent? Do you return like for like or remain humble and flexible, calm and peaceful?

Non-Competitive or Not Striving

Water benefits rather than rivals with everything.
— Tao Te Ching (Chapter 8)
Tao of the Sage is to act and not to strive.
— Tao Te Ching (Chapter 8

A proverb goes, "Better quit in time of success."
Some people become arrogant and complacent when
successful while others keep a low profile and even retire
when they are still at the height of their careers. To retire
or retain, to stay or quit, a wise man will make his
well-informed decision.
The stale gives way to the fresh. Fortune and
misfortune are interdependent. "One retires when
goals are attained." All these are acts that conform
to the Tao of Heaven.

A journey of a thousand miles begins with a single step

A big tree grows from a tiny sprout.
A nine-storey tower is built from the first basket of earth.
A journey of a thousand miles begins with a single step.
— Tao Te Ching (Chapter 64)

A great cause starts from trivial matters. Great men are no different from ordinary people when they were born. A grand goal requires solid efforts. "You cannot finish a thousand-mile journey without proceeding step by step; a river or sea will not come into existence without water from brooks and streams." This is the secret of high achievers.

Heaven and Earth Endure

The reason that they do so
Is that they do not live for themselves,
And thus they can endure.
— Tao Te Ching (Chapter 7)

The reason Heaven and Earth can exist for long is that they do not exist for themselves alone. It is our hope that all beautiful things will remain unchanged. However, nobody and nothing can endure as Heaven and Earth do, from the distant past through the present, from emperors to ordinary civilians, from noble houses to general families.

Low Positioning

Know the masculine, yet hold on to the feminine,
Be a valley for everyone. As the valley for everyone,
You'll have Virtue forever, and return to infancy.
— Tao Te Ching (Chapter 28)

Low positioning means to place oneself below
others or to be modest. As a French philosopher
says: "To make enemies, overtake your friends.
To make friends, let your friends overtake."

Empty and Silent

Attain the ultimate emptiness,
hold fast to a mind of peace.
— Tao Te Ching (Chapter 16)

The natural world moves in an inconstant manner. So does the human society. How to observe the transitory and recurrent changes with an empty and serene mind and fulfil our missions assigned by Tao in the midst of sound and fury? This requires us to contemplate and strive non-stop for the lofty realm of life and spirit.

Knowing Yourself

You are clever if you understand others,
You are wise if you know yourself.
— Tao Te Ching (Chapter 33)

On many occasions we
know that we are wrong,
Yet find it hard to face up to others' criticism.
Often we keep our eyes fixed on mistakes made by others.
We feel confident with the pressure on us relieved.
Yet when looking back on what we have achieved, we realise
we have not done much...

There is still a lot
for me to improve
on in this respect.

ZEN INSPIRATION

Zen is a way of creative living. In this book, you will find out about Zen in all its vitality and simplicity. Whatever it is about Zen that fascinates you – silent meditation or creative expression – you will not be disappointed as you dip into the pages of this book.
Illustrated by **Fu Chunjiang**. *224pp, 150x210mm, ISBN 981-229-455-4.*

INSPIRATION FROM CONFUCIUS:
Choice Quotations from the Analects

More than 100 choice quotations classified under broad themes depicting Confucian core values and enhanced by inspirational thoughts. With additional features on Confucius' life, achievements and influence, it makes an excellent representation of the *Analects*.
Illustrated by **Jeffrey Seow**. *224pp, 150x210mm, ISBN 981-229-398-1.*

THE TAO INSPIRATION :
Essence of Lao Zi's Wisdom

Written more than 2,500 years ago, the Tao Te Ching now comes in 21st century style. Presenting Lao Zi's masterpiece in a concise, comprehensive yet profound manner, this book provides practical wisdom for leadership and for achieving balance and harmony in everyday life.
Illustrated by **Feng Ge**. *176pp, 150x210mm, ISBN 981-229-396-5.*

THE ART OF PEACE

The perfect companion if daily stories on war and terrorism are tiring you out. Learn how Mo Zi spread his message of peace to warring states locked in endless conflicts and power struggles.
Illustrated by **Chan Kok Sing**, *152pp, 150x210mm, ISBN 981-229-390-6.*

道 的 启 示
— 老 子 的 智 慧 真 谛

绘画：冯戈

翻译：杨立平

亚太图书有限公司出版